Advances in AI for Financial, Cyber, and Healthcare Analytics: A Multidisciplinary Approach

Edited By

Ashwani Kumar

School of Computer Science Engineering and Technology
Bennett University, Greater Noida, India

Mohit Kumar

Department of Computer Science and Engineering
Amity University Ranchi– 834001 Jharkhand
India

Avinash Kumar Sharma

School of Engineering and Technology
Sharda University, Greater Noida, India

&

Yojna Arora

School of Engineering and Technology
Sharda University, Greater Noida, India

I0047507

Advances in AI for Financial, Cyber, and Healthcare Analytics: A Multidisciplinary Approach

Editors: Ashwani Kumar, Mohit Kumar, Avinash Kumar Sharma & Yojna Arora

ISBN (Online): 979-8-89881-054-2

ISBN (Print): 979-8-89881-055-9

ISBN (Paperback): 979-8-89881-056-6

© 2025, Bentham Books imprint.

Published by Bentham Science Publishers Pte. Ltd. Singapore, in collaboration with Eureka Conferences, USA. All Rights Reserved.

First published in 2025.

BENTHAM SCIENCE PUBLISHERS LTD.
End User License Agreement (for non-institutional, personal use)

This is an agreement between you and Bentham Science Publishers Ltd. Please read this License Agreement carefully before using the ebook/echapter/ejournal (**"Work"**). Your use of the Work constitutes your agreement to the terms and conditions set forth in this License Agreement. If you do not agree to these terms and conditions then you should not use the Work.

Bentham Science Publishers agrees to grant you a non-exclusive, non-transferable limited license to use the Work subject to and in accordance with the following terms and conditions. This License Agreement is for non-library, personal use only. For a library / institutional / multi user license in respect of the Work, please contact: permission@benthamscience.org.

Usage Rules:

1. All rights reserved: The Work is the subject of copyright and Bentham Science Publishers either owns the Work (and the copyright in it) or is licensed to distribute the Work. You shall not copy, reproduce, modify, remove, delete, augment, add to, publish, transmit, sell, resell, create derivative works from, or in any way exploit the Work or make the Work available for others to do any of the same, in any form or by any means, in whole or in part, in each case without the prior written permission of Bentham Science Publishers, unless stated otherwise in this License Agreement.
2. You may download a copy of the Work on one occasion to one personal computer (including tablet, laptop, desktop, or other such devices). You may make one back-up copy of the Work to avoid losing it.
3. The unauthorised use or distribution of copyrighted or other proprietary content is illegal and could subject you to liability for substantial money damages. You will be liable for any damage resulting from your misuse of the Work or any violation of this License Agreement, including any infringement by you of copyrights or proprietary rights.

Disclaimer:

Bentham Science Publishers does not guarantee that the information in the Work is error-free, or warrant that it will meet your requirements or that access to the Work will be uninterrupted or error-free. The Work is provided "as is" without warranty of any kind, either express or implied or statutory, including, without limitation, implied warranties of merchantability and fitness for a particular purpose. The entire risk as to the results and performance of the Work is assumed by you. No responsibility is assumed by Bentham Science Publishers, its staff, editors and/or authors for any injury and/or damage to persons or property as a matter of products liability, negligence or otherwise, or from any use or operation of any methods, products instruction, advertisements or ideas contained in the Work.

Limitation of Liability:

In no event will Bentham Science Publishers, its staff, editors and/or authors, be liable for any damages, including, without limitation, special, incidental and/or consequential damages and/or damages for lost data and/or profits arising out of (whether directly or indirectly) the use or inability to use the Work. The entire liability of Bentham Science Publishers shall be limited to the amount actually paid by you for the Work.

General:

1. Any dispute or claim arising out of or in connection with this License Agreement or the Work (including non-contractual disputes or claims) will be governed by and construed in accordance with the laws of Singapore. Each party agrees that the courts of the state of Singapore shall have exclusive jurisdiction to settle any dispute or claim arising out of or in connection with this License Agreement or the Work (including non-contractual disputes or claims).
2. Your rights under this License Agreement will automatically terminate without notice and without the

need for a court order if at any point you breach any terms of this License Agreement. In no event will any delay or failure by Bentham Science Publishers in enforcing your compliance with this License Agreement constitute a waiver of any of its rights.

3. You acknowledge that you have read this License Agreement, and agree to be bound by its terms and conditions. To the extent that any other terms and conditions presented on any website of Bentham Science Publishers conflict with, or are inconsistent with, the terms and conditions set out in this License Agreement, you acknowledge that the terms and conditions set out in this License Agreement shall prevail.

Bentham Science Publishers Pte. Ltd.
No. 9 Raffles Place
Office No. 26-01
Singapore 048619
Singapore
Email: subscriptions@benthamscience.net

BENTHAM
SCIENCE

CONTENTS

FOREWORD

In the past few years, the world of finance has experienced a seismic shift. Traditional financial analysis, relying heavily on historical data, human intuition, and static models, is now being supplemented, if not outright transformed, by the power of data science and machine learning. As financial markets continue to evolve in complexity and speed, the need for more sophisticated tools to analyze, predict, and optimize financial outcomes has never been greater. Against this background, machine learning for financial analytics emerges as a timely and necessary guide for professionals working within this new context. Financial data is best suited to machine learning techniques, as it possesses high volumes, variety, and velocity, characteristics that help identify patterns in large datasets, make predictions, and adapt to new information. From algorithmic trading to fraud detection, risk management to portfolio optimization, machine learning offers innovative solutions to some of the most pressing challenges in finance today. This book provides a comprehensive and approachable guide for those eager to harness the power of machine learning in the financial domain.

It also discusses how the techniques of machine learning could be used to provide new insights, improve forecasting, and optimize decisions in finance. The book easily navigates the challenges by giving the technical depth needed to understand the algorithms and the financial context necessary for their application. This is more than an academic resource; this is a practical guide to the future of finance. As we look forward, data-driven decision-making will continue to grow, and machine learning will be at the heart of this transformation. This book will provide you with the knowledge and tools needed to succeed in this fast-changing field if you are a financial analyst, a data scientist, an investor, or a student with an interest in the intersection of technology and finance. In the chapters that follow, you will embark on a journey that will reshape your understanding of both finance and machine learning.

Pradeep Kumar Gupta
Computer Science & Engineering and Information Technology
Jaypee University of Information Technology
Solan H.P, India

PREFACE

The intersection of machine learning (ML) and finance has emerged as a transformative force, reshaping the way financial professionals analyze markets, predict trends, and manage risks. As financial systems become increasingly complex and data-driven, traditional methods of analysis are no longer sufficient to handle the scale and intricacies of modern financial markets. Machine learning gives the ability to extract insights from vast datasets, identify patterns that may not be easily observed, and develop predictive models that inform decision-making for improved financial performance. This book will present an introduction to the application of machine learning techniques in financial analytics through an exploration of theoretical foundations and practical implementations in the subject area. We will examine core concepts of machine learning: supervised and unsupervised learning, as well as reinforcement learning. They will be applied in solutions to different financial problems, including the application of algorithmic trading, risk management, portfolio optimization, fraud detection, and market forecasting. As financial institutions and investment firms increasingly rely on data-driven insights to gain a competitive edge, the principles of machine learning have become essential for professionals looking to navigate the evolving landscape of financial analytics. This book aims to provide the reader with a broad view of how machine learning can be applied to solve real-world financial problems and the tools and techniques that need to be mastered to facilitate these solutions effectively.

In all chapters, we balance theory with practice by incorporating case studies, coding examples, and industry insights to guide the reader step by step in the process of designing, implementing, and evaluating machine learning models for financial analytics. Whether you are a financial analyst, data scientist, or a student eager to explore the vast potential of this exciting field, this book will serve as a valuable resource to help you build the knowledge and skills necessary to leverage machine learning in the financial sector. As the integration of technology and finance is becoming ever more intimate, machine learning is not only a tool but a paradigm for a new approach to financial analysis and decision-making. It is our hope that this book will inspire and equip you to engage with the dynamic field of financial analytics, unlocking new opportunities for innovation and growth.

Content and Organization

Chapter 1 explores how financial analytics is being revolutionized, transforming the ways institutions analyze data, manage risks, and make informed decisions. With the rapid growth in volume and complexity of financial data, machine learning enables organizations to uncover valuable insights and maintain a competitive edge. By leveraging advanced algorithms, financial firms can improve predictions, optimize investment strategies, and detect fraud more effectively. Nevertheless, challenges, such as ensuring data quality, dealing with non-stationary data, and enhancing model interpretability, must be addressed. Overcoming these obstacles is crucial to fully harnessing machine learning transformative potential in the financial sector and making it more transparent, adaptable, and reliable in dynamic environments.

Chapter 2 discusses that human activity recognition (HAR) helps in segregating and distinguishing human actions among data generated from numerous sensing modalities. In this review, an exploration of Deep Learning models for HAR is considered, focusing on advancements in CNN and LSTM architectures. Deep Learning models have considerably outperformed traditional machine learning approaches owing to their capacity for automatically extracting both spatial and temporal features. Furthermore, attention mechanisms, such as the self-attention and Squeeze and Excitation modules, have significantly enhanced model performance by focusing on relevant feature maps and recalibrating them adaptively. This review also highlights hybrid models that combine CNN and LSTM for more accurate HAR, especially when working with sensor-based datasets. Additionally, the incorporation of attention mechanisms not only boosts accuracy but also optimizes the complexity of the models. Key trends in attention-driven deep learning methods are examined, indicating their growing importance in real-world human activity recognition applications.

Chapter 3 provides the classification of acute leukemia and myeloid neoplasm using ResNet leverages deep learning for accurate diagnosis of hematological disorders. ResNet (Residual Network), a convolutional neural network architecture, is used to process microscopic blood smear images and classify cell abnormalities effectively. By utilizing residual connections, ResNet overcomes the vanishing gradient problem, enabling deep networks to learn complex features. This approach automates and improves diagnostic accuracy, reducing dependency on manual interpretation. The method is particularly effective for distinguishing between various subtypes of leukemia and myeloid neoplasms, aiding in early detection and personalized treatment strategies. Experimental results typically demonstrate high accuracy, showcasing the potential of ResNet in medical image analysis.

Chapter 4 examines the moral ramifications of AI decision-making in fields ranging from criminal justice and employment to healthcare and finance. There are numerous advantages to incorporating AI technologies into routine tasks, including improved accuracy and efficiency as well as data-driven insights. Algorithmic bias, which can result in discriminatory actions against minority groups, is one of the main issues discussed in this chapter. Since users and other affected parties frequently lack the knowledge necessary to refute the reasoning behind automated judgments, responsibility and trust have become increasingly prominent. Furthermore, where AI is at the crossroads of numerous human rights concerns, for instance, invasion of privacy and potential debasement of civil liberties, society faces direct challenges.

Chapter 5 deals with anticipating cyber threats using AI predictive learning as a proactive cybersecurity strategy. AI analyzes data, detects patterns, and raises alerts for emerging risks. Known attacks are handled with signature-based identification, while real-time monitoring, data preprocessing, and continuous learning improve threat detection. Machine Learning algorithms, anomaly detection, and behavioral analysis strengthen the system's predictive ability. This approach adapts to changing threats, safeguarding sensitive information and public trust while reducing risks. This concept aligns with "machine learning for financial analytics," as both fields use data-driven models for prediction. In finance, ML analyzes market trends and detects anomalies to predict risks. Similarly, AI in cybersecurity uses pattern recognition to predict and counter threats. Both fields depend on real-time data analysis, pattern detection, and continuous adaptation.

Chapter 6 explores IoT as a technique for smart home authentication. IoT refers to a network of physical objects, also known as "things," that are embedded with electronics, software, and other technologies that enable them to communicate and exchange data with one another and with other connected devices and systems over a network, such as the Internet [1]. In recent years, the Internet of Things has emerged as one of the most significant technological advancements. Due to its increasing popularity, IoT has become increasingly prominent in ordinary day-to-day activities and applications.

Chapter 7 discusses channel response measurements and analyzes the human body as a medium for biometric applications. Today, digital systems control every facet of human life, allowing more individuals to get the services they need through a variety of channels. Personal identification of smart devices based on biometric recognition, which uses an individual's unique biological characteristics to verify their identity, has become a viable option in recent years.

Chapter 8 deals with artificial intelligence (AI), which improves cybersecurity by offering advanced tools to detect and mitigate threats with efficiency. AI-enabled security systems analyse large volumes of data in real-time and recognize suspicious patterns. Machine learning-based models enable proactive threat detection by continuously learning from historical attack patterns. The proposed work contributes to understanding the role of AI in safeguarding digital ecosystems. The key contribution is its focus on AI's role in securing IoT environments, and scalable solutions to security. This chapter not only advances theoretical knowledge but also offers valuable insights into integrating AI with existing security frameworks. Ultimately, it serves as a roadmap for using AI in the building of defences against emerging cyber threats.

Ashwani Kumar
School of Computer Science Engineering and Technology
Bennett University, Greater Noida, India

Mohit Kumar
Department of Computer Science and Engineering
Amity University Ranchi– 834001
Jharkhand
India

Avinash Kumar Sharma
School of Engineering and Technology
Sharda University, Greater Noida
India

&

Yojna Arora
School of Engineering and Technology
Sharda University, Greater Noida
India

List of Contributors

Ajeet Kumar Sharma Department of CSE, Sharda University, Greater Noida, India

A. Aminu Sharda School of Engineering & Technology, Sharda University, Greater Noida, Uttar Pradesh, India

Arun Prakash Agarwal School of Computer Science Engineering & Technology, Bennett University, Greater Noida, Uttar Pradesh, India

Arvind Kumar Department of CSE, NSUT, Delhi 110031, India

Akshat Gautam Department of CSE, Sharda University, Greater Noida, India

B.S. Kiruthika Devi School of Computing, Sathyabama Institute of Science and Technology, Chennai, India

Esha Singh Department of CSE, Sharda University, Greater Noida, India

Gaurav Kumar Department of Computer Science and Application, School of Computer Science and Engineering, IILM University, Greater Noida, India

Gowroju Swathi Department of Computer Science and Engineering (AI and ML), Sreyas Institute of Engineering and Technology, Nagole, Hyderabad, India

G. Jyothi Department of Computer Science and Engineering (DS), Sreyas Institute of Engineering and Technology, Nagole, India

G. J. Lakshmi Department of ECE, Aditya University, Surampalem, India

Jyoti Gautam Department of CSE, NSUT, Delhi 110031, India

Kumar G. Arun Department of Electronics & Communication Engg., JSS Academy of Technical Education, Noida, Uttar Pradesh, India

Kirti Sharma Department of CSE, NSUT, Delhi 110031, India

Komal Shakya Department of CSE, Sharda University, Greater Noida, India

Mahadev Ajagalla School of Computer Science Engineering and Technology, Bennett University, Greater Noida, Uttar Pradesh, India

Mahesh K. Singh Department of ECE, Aditya University, Surampalem, India

M. S. Priya Department of ECE, Aditya University, Surampalem, India

Rosey Chauhan Department Of Computer Science and Engineering, Sharda University, Greater Noida, India

Rajneesh Kumar Singh Sharda School of Engineering & Technology, Sharda University, Greater Noida, Uttar Pradesh, India

Raj Shekhar School of Computer Science Engineering and Technology, Bennett University, Greater Noida, Uttar Pradesh, India

Sarvesh Maurya School of Computer Science Engineering and Technology, Bennett University, Greater Noida, Uttar Pradesh, India

S. Pratap Singh Thapar Institute of Engineering and Technology, Patiala, Punjab, India

Srivash A. Department Of Computer Science and Engineering, Sharda University, Greater Noida, India

Shikha Chadha   Department Of Computer Science and Engineering, Sharda University, Greater Noida, India

Shobha Bhatt   Department of CSE, NSUT, Delhi 110031, India

Sanjeev Kumar   Department of ECE, Aditya University, Surampalem, India

V. Satyanarayana   Department of ECE, Aditya University, Surampalem, India

CHAPTER 1

Introduction to Financial Analytics and Machine Learning

Raj Shekhar[1,*], **Sarvesh Maurya**[1] and **Mahadev Ajagalla**[1]

[1] *School of Computer Science Engineering and Technology, Bennett University, Greater Noida, Uttar Pradesh, India*

Abstract: This chapter will introduce financial analytics very holistically and then dive into how machine learning transformed the finance industry. The discussion shall start with the underlying principles of financial analytics; it involves rigorous analytical expositions of financial data to deduce insights that promote decision-making, enhance performance, and avoid risks. Areas such as performance analysis, risk management, forecasting, fraud detection, and optimization will be featured within this light theme of data-driven decision-making in contemporary finance. The role of machine learning is then discussed within the chapter. The author states that the impact machine learning <u>has</u> on predictive analytics, algorithmic trading, fraud detection, portfolio optimization, and scoring credit has increased lately. Much more accurate and almost instantaneous decision-making with financial applications is enabled by machine learning when processing large, complex datasets. A challenge to financial data, the chapter goes on to discuss issues it poses in terms of quality, non-stationarity, imbalanced datasets, and interpretability of model outcomes. While such challenges are plentiful, there are many opportunities as well inside this landscape, from alternative sources of data to real-time analytics, automation, and even RegTech solutions. The chapter concludes by stating that it is only when the following challenges are addressed that machine learning will truly be leveraged in finance for both scalable insight and cooperative intelligence.

Keywords: Financial analytics, Machine learning, Principal component analysis.

INTRODUCTION

Financial analytics refers to the entirety of finance data analysis with the aim of creating meaningful insights into decision-making, the improvement of financial performance, and risk control. This is a systematic process that involves the examination of several financial metrics-based assessments of the financial health of an organization, such as revenue, expenditures, profit margins, and investment returns. Financial analytics leads to corporations' use of historical data in

---

*Corresponding author **Raj Shekhar**: School of Computer Science Engineering and Technology, Bennett University, Greater Noida, Uttar Pradesh, India; E-mail: raj.shekhar@bennett.edu.in

Ashwani Kumar, Mohit Kumar, Avinash Kumar Sharma & Yojna Arora (Eds.)
All rights reserved-© 2025 Bentham Science Publishers

determining and predicting business trends and future outcomes. It supports crucial areas such as budgeting, forecasting, and resource allocation by helping organizations make decisions based on data towards improving profitability and increasing efficiency. Another important role played by financial analytics [1 - 4] is its implication in risk management, which yields the identification of potential financial risks associated with the organization's actions and finding ways to minimize these risks. This analytical process equips businesses with tools and insights to adapt to the changing market conditions and to make informed investment choices that guarantee their long-term financial sustainability. Key areas in financial analytics include:

Performance Analysis

Performance analysis is a critical function of financial analytics: assessing what companies, or their portfolios and assets, have performed over time and thereby helps evaluate the efficiency of operations, profitability, and overall financial health of a company. Basic metrics applied in performance evaluation are Return on Investment, ROI, which provides the profit obtained from an investment relative to its cost and therefore allows the investor to make decisions on the efficiency of an investment relative to others and their profitability; Earnings Before Interest and Taxes, EBIT, which indicates a company's operational earnings beyond the influence of financial structure for comparisons within an industry; and profit margins, gross, operating, and net, which measure the extent of revenues retained as profits at different stages in operations. Higher margins mean effective control over costs and prices. Moreover, metrics such as Return on Equity (ROE) measure the return yielded on the shareholders' equity, thus making it a richer analysis. Collectively formed in that organizations use these metrics to analyze their financial position, make better decisions regarding investment choices, and find areas that present opportunities for improvement.

Risk Management

Financial operations risk management involves the systematic identification, quantification, and mitigation of risks that might adversely affect a firm's financial stability and performance. There exist different types of risks, which include credit risk, market risk, and operational risk, all of which require specific strategies to be in place to manage these risks effectively. Credit risk is believed to be the risk generated by the probability of defaulting of a borrower in the discharge of his duties. In relation to the handling of this risk, financial institutions consider creditworthiness and operate within appropriate lending limits. Market risk arises as a result of losses to finance resulting from changes in other market variables like interest rates, exchange rates, or stock prices and is generally addressed using hedging and diversification. It relates to risks from internal failures-which include system and human failures-and external events, which are managed through robust internal controls, audit, and contingency planning. Machine learning and advanced analytics continue to assume critical roles in risk management through their enablers, including voluminous data analysis, the identification of emerging risks in real time, and dynamic adjustments of strategies to quickly minimize losses. Through these quantitative models combined with human expertise, a firm will be able to assess how exposed they are to risk and, therefore, put in place specific controls to protect their financial interests.

Forecasting and Prediction

Forecasting and prediction [5, 6] are essential components of financial analytics that leverage historical data to anticipate future financial outcomes, enabling organizations to make informed decisions and optimize resource allocation. By analyzing past trends, financial analysts can predict stock prices, market trends, and consumer behaviours, which are crucial for strategic planning. For instance, in stock price prediction, various statistical and machine learning techniques are employed to analyze historical data and macroeconomic indicators, aiding investors in making buy, hold, or sell decisions. Additionally, forecasting plays a vital role in budgeting and cash flow management, as organizations use historical financial data to create realistic budgets and predict future cash inflows and outflows, ensuring sufficient liquidity for operations. Revenue prediction, similarly, involves analyzing sales data and market conditions to estimate future revenue streams, helping businesses set targets and identify growth opportunities. Techniques such as time series analysis, regression analysis, and machine learning models enhance the accuracy of these forecasts by identifying patterns and relationships in data. Overall, effective forecasting and prediction empower organizations to navigate financial complexities, allocate resources wisely, and position themselves for success in a dynamic market environment.

Optimization

Optimization is a crucial aspect of financial analytics that aims to identify the most efficient ways to allocate resources, maximizing returns while minimizing risks and costs. One primary application is portfolio optimization, where financial analysts utilize Modern Portfolio Theory (MPT) to select the ideal combination of assets, diversifying investments across various classes like stocks, bonds, and real estate to achieve an optimal risk-return balance. Additionally, investment balancing involves continuously monitoring and adjusting portfolios to maintain desired risk levels, ensuring that changing market conditions and asset performances do not lead to excessive risk exposure. Debt management also benefits from optimization strategies, allowing organizations to analyze their debt structure, refinance, or consolidate debt effectively, thereby minimizing borrowing costs and enhancing financial stability. Various quantitative methods, including linear programming and stochastic optimization, are employed to solve these problems, while advancements in machine learning and artificial intelligence further enhance optimization processes by analyzing large datasets and identifying complex patterns. Overall, optimization enables organizations to make strategic, data-driven decisions that improve financial performance and ensure long-term sustainability in an ever-evolving financial landscape.

This wide field of financial analytics involves a wide range of tools and techniques, empowering financial professionals to be able to manage large amounts of financial data with insights that would be relevant to making decisions, as shown in Fig. (**1**). The most important part is, of course, the statistical analysis: several methods are used to summarize, interpret, and draw conclusions about data, which allow analysts to identify trends, correlations, and anomalies. On the other hand, econometrics uses statistical methods to present models that might describe relationships or linkages between variables and predict future financial performances. Moreover, users can easily understand and make analyses if complicated data is presented in an understandable manner, while data visualization tools make the interpretation easier. Charts, graphs, and dashboards are all used to pinpoint important metrics and trends but then quickly facilitate choices for all stakeholders. Other techniques could include predictive modelling using machine learning algorithms, frameworks to assess risk with uncertainties quantified, and simulation tools to test various financial scenarios [7]. The above tools and techniques are designed to enable the financial professional to make effective decisions, enhance operational efficiency, and inform strategic plans for investments, managing risk and performance appraisals by turning raw data into meaningful insights.

TYPES OF FINANCIAL DATA

Financial data forms the basis for applying analytical techniques and algorithms to drive insights, predictions, and decision-making.

Time Series Data

Financial time series data represent a set of data indexed in chronological order, capturing the evolution over time of financial variables. Examples include stock price data and exchange rate data, determining great importance when understanding market behaviour and the economy. These data are highly useful for financial modelling and forecasting and providing the analyst with the capacity to find trends, seasonal effects, and trends over very long periods for use in decision-making. Any future values can be forecasted using past time series data through various time series analysis techniques such as moving averages, exponential smoothing, and ARIMA models. These methods enable the determination of cycle patterns and volatility, thus enlightening market dynamics and efficient risk management. Time series data [8 - 12] is important in building legitimate algorithms of trading, the evaluation of investment, or scenario analysis since only through this approach is it possible to estimate how past events can affect future financial outcomes in terms of time and date. Therefore, it leads to an overall foundation of analyzing time series data in finance, driving the insights behind practical investment strategies and general financial improvement.

Fig. (1). Machine learning in finance.

Transactional Data

Transactional data contains all the minute details of financial transactions, which may include credit card payments, loan disbursements, trade data, and other financial activities for a certain period of time. This type of data will, therefore, help an organization have granular insights about the customer spending pattern or cash flows, thereby enabling analysis of how customers are interacting with the financial products being offered by them. Analyzing transactional data reveals patterns in buying habits and sets up the efficiency of their campaign to promote marketing. Eventually, the data helps them know customer preferences and better design or tailor the product to meet the needs of the market. This information also plays a critical role in cash flow management since it helps in tracking inflows and outflows, predicting future requirements, and using funds appropriately in terms of budgeting and investment. Beyond these insights, the analysis of transactional data may also involve anomalies that assist companies in detecting fraud efficiently and further risk management. Here, the bottom line is that transactional data represents an essentially valuable resource for any financial analytics. Organizations can derive actionable insights into their customers' interactions, optimize operational efficiency, and, ultimately, make strategic decisions to maintain leadership within the competitive game in the financial marketplace.

Macroeconomic Data

These are Gross Domestic Product, inflation rates, unemployment rates, and interest rates, all of which together give an overview of the general state of an economy. They are helpful in analyzing the macroeconomic backdrop under which the financial markets operate because it affects investment decisions, consumer behaviours, and government policies. For instance, GDP is considered one of the basic indicators of the level of economic activity in a country and reflects the total value of goods and services produced inside a country. In addition, GDP could measure growth or shrinkage in an economy. A country's inflation rate measures the trend over time that has caused the prices to rise, reducing the purchasing power. Inflation, therefore, influences the central bank's decisions about interest rates in that it affects the cost of borrowing and consumer spending. Unemployment rates, for instance, signify the deeper labor market conditions that would have a bearing on consumer confidence as well as spending capacity. In this regard, macro-economic data is used by analysts and financial experts to gauge the forward-market trend of markets, assess risks, and plan investments. In fact, interpreting such indicators of the economy in correlation with the performance of financial markets helps understand better possible market moves and makes informed decisions in line with reality. Macro data forms a very integral part of financial analytics as it guides short-term and long-term financial planning in today's ever-changing economic landscape.

Alternative Data

Alternative data refers to non-traditional data sources that provide unique insights to complement and support the effectiveness of financial analytics. Some examples of alternative data are social media sentiment, satellite imagery, web traffic, and other unconventional datasets. For example, whereas social media sentiment analysis enables the monitoring of public perception about a brand or product, it offers rich information regarding consumer behaviour and likely shifts in the market well ahead of these in conventional financial reports. Satellite imaging can record retail foot traffic or agricultural crop yield, enabling analysts to gauge in real-time how well a company is performing or what supply of a commodity exists. Furthermore, web traffic data can even be used to reflect consumer interest and engagement in products or services and thus represent an early market trend indicator. In this regard, alternative data can be very helpful for making a competitive advantage over the identification of hidden opportunities and risks that other more traditional data sources might overlook. This approach enhances the accuracy of the forecasting of the firms, but at the same time, it allows firms to respond much more agilely to changes in the marketplace, which ultimately helps push better investment and strategic initiatives in such an increasingly complex financial landscape. Financial analytics helps stakeholders—including investors, regulators, and corporate decision-makers—assess their financial standing, make investment decisions, and manage risks effectively [13 - 17].

ROLE OF MACHINE LEARNING IN FINANCE

Machine learning transforms the financial sector. Traditional methods of analysis may not automatically process large, complicated datasets and related information elements in large volumes as promptly or accurately as machine learning. It can be used in nearly every application that is in use in finance to deliver effective predictive models, real-time anomaly detection, and real-time decision-making.

Key Applications of Machine Learning in Finance:

Predictive Analytics

Predictive analytics leverages machine learning (ML), particularly time-series models, to forecast financial outcomes such as stock market prices and economic changes. Machine learning algorithms thereby expose patterns and potential relationships that could be good predictors of future trends in the markets while in the course of analyzing past data. Recent techniques have included the application of neural networks and deep learning algorithms in the formation of sophisticated models to predict the prices of stocks. Recurrent neural networks and long short-term memory models are designed with sequential dependency capture in mind, making them more suitable for usage in the analysis of financial time series data. Its predictive analytics capability becomes a deep learning model since it can automatically learn complex data representation and, thus, discover hidden patterns not attainable through statistical methods. The models improve with time as they continue to be exposed to new data streams; for example, they can adjust to market environment changes. The use of these advanced techniques gives financial institutions a chance to make better decisions on investment and anticipate market trends, thereby optimising the strategies applicable in investment [18, 19].

Risk Management

Modern risk management works intensively because of machine learning to identify patterns in huge datasets which are actually exposed to market volatility, credit, or operational risks. In contrast, traditional risk management depends on static models and old information, yet, machine learning updates this process dynamically by analyzing huge structured and unstructured datasets and realizing new, subtle correlations and trends that foretell emerging risks. For example, in market risk, ML models can forecast periods of volatile increase based on the analysis of prevailing market behavior, sentiment data, and macroeconomic factors. In credit risk, such models calculate the probability of default for the borrower based on many parameters, including transaction history, alternative data such as social media behavior, and economic conditions, hence facilitating increasingly accurate and individualized risk assessment. In the case of operational risk, machine learning enables organizations to track internal processes, identify inefficiencies, and even detect potential threats like fraud or system failure due to analyzing data streams in real time. Adaptability is one of the key benefits of machine learning in the context of risk management; these models learn by constantly incorporating new data and thus change the systems to better assess real situations related to risky conditions in the market. This dynamic capability allows organizations to leap and anticipate the risk by means of proactive strategy, making their risk management strong and responsive to the evolving nature of financial landscapes [13, 20].

Algorithmic Trading

Algorithmic trading, equipped with machine learning (ML) algorithms, has completely changed the dynamics of financial market operations as it allows trades to be executed at extraordinary speeds and much more precision. These ML-based algorithms can easily run through an abyss of market data and detect arbitrage opportunities—the temporary price inefficiencies between two different markets or assets—which might elude human traders at the moment. This means that algorithmic trading will use the lack of deviation in real time to optimize trade execution, including determining the best possible trade price and minimizing transaction costs. Furthermore, ML algorithms learn and fine-tune their trading strategies according to new incoming data streams; this makes them very adaptable to market conditions. Therefore, this adaptability makes algorithmic trading quite effective in dealing with the short-term form of movement of prices where little chances of quick gains over time may add up. Analysis of patterns, sentiment, and other market signals allows these algorithms to predict such price shifts and often execute thousands of trades in mere seconds to capture such time-sensitive opportunities. Besides speed and accuracy, ML algorithms [3] provide better liquidity and market efficiency as they further encourage high-speed trade and decrease reliance on human intervention. In short, the infusion of machine learning into trading algorithms gives traders a competitive advantage, optimized strategies with minimized costs, with no sacrifice in timeliness and efficiency against fast-changing financial markets.

Fraud Detection

Machine learning enhances the ability to identify unusual transaction patterns, which could indicate fraudulent behaviour such as high or low transaction volume or frequency, occurrence in unusual locations, and aberrant behavioural patterns. Traditional fraud detection systems rely on strict rules; hence, their adaptation to new and evolved fraud tactics is limited. These kinds of machine learning models allow analyzing enormous volumes of transactional data; in many such cases, they could find anomalies imperceptible by humans or even traditional rule-based systems. In this case, machine learning models learn from historical transaction data, building up the distinction between normal and suspicious behavior. Thus, a model, for example, may notice a sudden jump in spending or an unusual transaction from a foreign country flagged by the model as a potential fraud because of learned patterns from previous fraudulent cases. When trained, these models continue to improve with the addition of further data, now increasingly sophisticated in identifying new techniques of fraud [16]. The strength of machine learning lies in its ability to detect fraud in real-time, enabling financial institutions to block or flag suspicious transactions almost instantly and prevent losses before they occur. To continue analyzing new data and adjust against changing fraud patterns, a robust and scalable solution for boosting security while minimizing the risks of fraud is achieved through machine learning-based fraud detection systems.

Portfolio Optimization

This is because machine learning optimizes portfolios, providing strategies for an asset allocation that yields a maximum amount of return while reducing as much risk as possible. Portfolio management today depends on traditional methods, such as historical data and unchanging models that do not adjust to market conditions. However, this can be totally done based on real-time market conditions using techniques like reinforcement learning. Their algorithms in reinforcement learning continue to learn from the consequences of their actions, such that they are adjusting investment strategies according to fluctuating market environments. They may model a vast set of scenarios that is possible in the market and judge overall risks while rebalancing asset portfolios for maximum performance. For example, when the markets are unstable, machine-learning algorithms can shift the investments to more secure assets to minimize losses, while in stable conditions, they can emphasize more riskier - higher-reward assets. This ability to constantly update and refine based on the latest data enables risk management to be more precise, capital allocation more efficient, and much more. Machine learning can also accept many datasets-including macroeconomic indicators, social sentiment, and alternative data to make better decisions. In this regard, machine learning helps in portfolio management through the provision of dynamic, data-driven approaches for striking the perfect balance between risk and return, enabling investors to better respond to market shifts and take advantage of emerging opportunities.

Sentiment Analysis

In finance, sentiment analysis uses machine learning models to measure market sentiment in words from a source like news articles, social media posts, financial reports [21], and other public communications. The models evaluate the tone, emotion, and overall sentiment posed from such sources to classify whether the market sentiment is positive, negative, or neutral. An upward movement in positive news or social media discussions about any company or industry could highlight potential growth or upswings in stock prices, whereas negative news would highlight potential downfall or increased risk. Machine learning algorithms are trained to capture very subtle language patterns and can even interpret nuances of text like sarcasm or context-specific jargon and give a more accurate estimation of what's afoot in public opinion. These models, by processing vast amounts of real-time data, have the capability to detect the shifts in sentiment that might occur prior to an actual market movement, thus providing investors with insight into the likely impact of such public perceptions on financial markets. Sentiment analysis is a very powerful tool in predictive analytics, which allows traders and financial analysts to introduce emotion and psychological overtones into their decision-making processes to make an investment strategy much timelier and more accurate in response to the sentiment of people.

Customer Experience Enhancement

With the help of this burgeoning technology called machine learning, financial companies can now increase their relationship with the customer and provide more personal interactions and specifically tailored financial products, such as loans, insurance, and investments, based upon individual profiles and preferences. The best part of this model is it sifts through many volumes of data related to a customer's behavior, transaction history, demographics, or even social media activities to detect patterns and predict those needs with good accuracy. For instance, the algorithm may recommend specific loan products to a customer who wants to purchase a house or some customized investment portfolio depending on the amount of risk the customer is willing to accept and his or her financial objectives. Such stages of personalization are high in satisfaction levels because they depend on relevance and the timeliness of offers experienced by the customer, and thus, interactions are meaningful as well as efficient. More importantly, since machine learning models can continuously learn and adapt to changing customer preferences, it goes without saying that recommendations become current and up-to-date because of the continuous change in customer behavior [22]. However, aside from product recommendation, the current applications of machine learning are also promising for the streamlining of customer service through AI chatbots and virtual assistants addressing customers instantly for further experience enhancement. This would personalize an approach that not only could make relationships better but also increase engagement, loyalty, and, ultimately, the profitability of financial institutions based on these needs.

CHALLENGES AND OPPORTUNITIES IN FINANCIAL DATA

While machine learning offers many opportunities in finance, there are several challenges that need to be addressed to ensure the success and accuracy of these models.

Challenges in Financial Data

Data Quality and Availability

Financial data are mostly noisy, or incomplete, and outdated by their nature, which makes the financial analytic space challenging in terms of data quality and availability. Thus, the quality of a machine learning model is directly proportional to the quality of data on which the model is built; hence, the need for superior quality relevant data to build models that yield accurate predictions and actionable insights is imminent. However, financial data sets often contain missing values [8], errors, or inconsistencies due to a number of factors, for instance, data entry errors, system failure, or changes in reporting standards. For instance, an incomplete transaction record can alter the whole dataset, thereby causing incorrect analyses and wrong decisions. In addition, older data can no longer represent the present scenario, thereby causing strategies that may no longer be relevant or applicable. Such issues not only make difficult modeling but also give rise to biases that could adversely affect outcomes from financial analyses. Organisations have to use a lot of time and resources cleaning the data, validating it, and preprocessing the data to ensure that they are working with clean data sets. When the data quality issues identified herein are not mitigated, financial institutions run a massive risk of making decisions based on some and significant inaccuracies, and therefore, large financial losses and reputational damage can occur. High-quality data thus has to be maintained for applying machine learning in financial contexts.

High Dimensionality

Indeed, the issue of high dimensionality-one implying many variables or features in the problem statement that would bog down the modeling process indeed poses one of the great challenges in financial data analytics. Indeed, when datasets start becoming increasingly complex, the dimensionality of a problem can lead to overfitting such that a model learns the noise rather than the underlying signal. Such complexity can be managed effectively only by feature selection or dimensionality reduction techniques One such technique is feature selection, in which only the variables most relevant to the model's predictive performance are chosen, simplifying the dataset without significant loss of information. Techniques like PCA transform the original high-dimensional data into a lower-dimensional space that captures the most critical variance in the data and discards less informative features. It is helpful for reducing the high computational cost and interpretation or working with models that possibly are good at avoiding "the curse of dimensionality," which often results in very poor generalization on unknown data. Using such techniques, financial analysts will be able to take more significant conclusions from their datasets: more accurate forecasting and truly informed decisions in an environment where grasping many entangled relationships is the key to successful financial strategies.

Non-Stationarity

One of the challenges for financial analytics is non-stationarity. When financial markets change dynamically over time, it makes them volatile, and statistical properties like mean, variance, and correlation may become time-dependent; thus, models learned from a training set may not apply to a test set if they depict changes in market condition. For example, a model built with the aid of the data gathered in the stable phase of the economy will operate poorly during a crisis or at the onset of a crisis period, as the relations between the major variables are totally changed. Hence, non-stationarity models are likely to be misled by out-of-date patterns that no longer have relevance and thus make wrong predictions and bad investment decisions. Techniques to model time series have to consider mechanisms that actually notice changes in the underlying distribution of the data and update to accommodate changes. Thus, adaptive learning is central to this process since models are constantly updated for new parameters and learned from new data as it comes in. Thus, with adaptive algorithms that are responsive to changes in the dynamics of market experience, financial analysts [23] can improve on the strength of their forecasting models so that they maintain their relevance and accuracy overtime. From this perspective, therefore, not only do forecasts become more reliable, but the financial institutions, in turn, find it easier to handle the vagaries of the market towards have superior decision-making within this dynamic financial environment.

Imbalanced Data

Imbalanced data is one of the major challenges in many financial applications, especially when dealing with fraud detection and bankruptcy prediction; the classes tend to be imbalanced. This may happen when instances of fraud in a financial transaction dataset represent only a tiny fraction of the total records, thereby making it an imbalanced dataset. This skewing poses a high risk because traditional models of learning for typical traditional models optimize global accuracy at the expense of deviation from the majority class. Therefore, such models would likely fail to identify a small number of critical cases, like fraudulent activity, which may go unnoticed under the vast number of honest transactions. It will then incur heavy financial costs and reputational risk coupled with heightened vulnerability to other dangers for financial organizations when infrequent instances are comprised of unidentified events. Some key techniques used in handling imbalanced data include resampling methods such as oversampling the minority class as well as undersampling the majority class, cost-sensitive learning, and the use of anomaly detection algorithms. Implementation of these approaches enables financial analysts to increase the sensitivity and specificity of models to be more responsive to the most important yet relatively rare cases that otherwise may be missed. Effective handling of imbalanced data will improve accuracy and reliability in predictive models in the financial sector, enabling institutions to protect against fraud and make wise decisions regarding risk management [4].

Overfitting

Overfitting is a problem that is easily found in complex financial systems that involve large volumes of data; a model suffers from overfitting the training data if it picks noise and some specific patterns that do not generalize well to new, unseen data. As a result, the model becomes poor at prediction under real-world application. Overfitting represents a severe risk in financial analytics, wherein the consequences of inaccuracy in predictions are quite pronounced; overfit models might present misleading representations of the underlying relationships between variables. Such a scenario could be worsened with the high dimensionality of financial datasets, where there are so many features that obscure meaningful patterns and contribute to overfitting the model into the training data. Overfitting can be avoided through numerous strategies, such as cross-validation. That is, the creation of the training and the validation sets of the data will find out how well the model performs on different subsets, thus ensuring that it generalizes well to different data points. Regularization techniques also come in handy in terms of imposing penalties against models that are overly complex, thus preferring simpler representations less prone to fitting the training data. That is, pruning algorithms can be applied to the decision tree or even neural networks to eliminate nodes that contribute the least towards the model's ability to give predictions. Such measures will place the financial analyst in a great position to construct a robust and reliable machine learning model such that its strength is upheld when adapted to new data, thus allowing accurate prediction and decision-making to be facilitated within the real-world financial environment [14].

Interpretability and Transparency

Interpretability and transparency have been paramount for this financial sector mainly due to regulatory and compliance needs that require explanations for decisions made by machine learning models. With such high stakes-on one hand, the trust of consumers and on the other, scrutiny from the regulators-the predictive models employed within these financial institutions must provide correct output while also explaining the rationale behind their conclusions. However, most machine learning algorithms, particularly deep models, are treated as "black boxes" because they rely on intricate structures that are undecipherable. This is rather a challenge in the regulatory arena because end-users need a good insight into the variables affecting the outputs of such models. Techniques for explainable artificial intelligence, therefore, come increasingly applied to unravel what is happening inside these models. Certain specialized XAI methods like LIME and SHAP allow for the explicit highlighting of which individual features contribute to the predictions of a model, thus shedding light on precisely why certain decisions were made. Hence, with the interpretability of models, financial institutions can not only fulfill their regulatory requirements but also enhance accountability and trust amongst their customers and regulators. In addition, increased transparency allows organizations to be able to establish whether there is bias in their models; hence, even though they are productive applications, by producing effective financial solutions, they are ethically sound. From this regard, a balance between innovation in machine learning and placing in it the necessary safeguards that are inherent in the financial sector calls for the incorporation of measures on interpretability and transparency.

Opportunities in Financial Data

Alternative Data Sources

The data becomes a revolutionary opportunity at the financial sector level, where the institutions can gain a competitive advantage by leveraging the nontraditional information that goes beyond the conventional datasets. Therefore, among such sources of alternative data include satellite imagery, credit card transactions, social media sentiment, and web traffic analytics sources which present unique insights to amplify predictive capabilities in financial modelling. For instance, satellite imagery may be useful in evaluating farm yields or tracking the footfalls at retail channels of some specific categories that help yield real-time indicators of economic activity that otherwise could not have been readily inferred from traditional sources of data. Similarly, credit card transactions can be analyzed to track consumers' spending patterns and trends by financial analysts, while the use of social media will help gauge public perception and its possible influence on the movement of markets through sentiment analysis. Financial institutions will thereby integrate all forms of data into the frameworks of their analysis and develop more sophisticated and more predictive models for both the trends in markets and consumer behavior as well as macroeconomic indicators. At the same time, integration will enrich the analytical landscape and make sound investment decisions and assessments of risk. The continued evolution of the landscape of financial data will make alternative data crucial for firms trying to maintain a competitive edge in such an increasingly competitive market, thus enabling them to respond sooner rather than later to changes in dynamics and capture emerging opportunities faster [15].

Real-time Analytics

Real-time analytics has revolutionized the financial world by allowing immediate processing of data, which has become a key determinant in making decisions in a dynamically changing market environment within an instant. This is very crucial for algorithmic trading where transactions occur within microsecond speeds, and analysis of huge amounts of data must be made quickly to identify available trades as ideally suited for execution before market conditions change. This is an instance where advanced algorithms combined with high-frequency trading strategies allow financial institutions to exploit transient arbitrage opportunities and market inefficiencies to create a greater competitive advantage. Real-time analytics also plays a critical role in fraud detection because it makes it possible to track transactional patterns continuously and highlight suspicious transactions in real-time. For instance, by combining machine learning algorithms that analyze historical transaction data with current inputs in real-time, financial systems can establish anomaly patterns about sudden spikes in transaction volumes or geographical anomalies and alert users immediately to opportunities for thwarted frauds. Real-time analytics of finance operations improve operational efficiency but also enhance the capabilities for risk management, which helps organizations respond swiftly to either threats or opportunities in the marketplace. With the transactions made in financial markets accelerating rapidly, institutions would be better positioned to correctly navigate modern financial markets if they could harness the power of real-time analytics [16].

Automation and Efficiency

The use of machine learning has greatly improved the automation and efficiency of financial operations and streamlined lots of processes by decreasing the amount of manual intervention required in different operations. There is no better example than the recent rise of robo-advisors, who use sophisticated algorithms to offer automated investment advice that is customized to individual client profiles and financial goals. Such platforms can thus leverage machine learning [24 - 26] to analyze large datasets, such as historical market trends, an individual's tolerance for risk, and his or her investment preferences. Optimized investment portfolios can thus be produced with the minimum amount of human oversight. This allows clients to receive individualized advice for a fraction of the cost usually charged by traditional financial advisors while democratizing access to high-quality strategies that had remained the preserve of wealthier individuals hitherto. Robo-advisors are always working hard, and the changes in the market keep upgrading; they reallocate assets and continuously monitor performance in real-time. This results in improving the overall client experience. What is more, this kind of automatic handling of routine tasks enables financial professionals to focus their attention on other strategic initiatives, leading to a lot more innovation within financial institutions. The ability to drive further automation and efficiency in financial services will, therefore, be reshaped by the further evolution of machine learning and will allow organizations to operate better while delivering greater value to clients.

RegTech

This type of technology is referred to as RegTech, and it primarily uses advanced data analytics and machine learning technologies. This enhances the efficiency and effectiveness with which financial institutions are able to undertake regulatory processes. It automates compliance checks on critical requirements like AML and KYC, allowing firms to save some massive amounts of money that they would otherwise spend in availing adherence to the regulatory requirements. These technologies apply sophisticated algorithms in order to analyze huge heaps of data and identify patterns and anomalies that may point to non-compliance or potentially fraudulent activities. For instance, a machine learning model can be trained to flag suspicious transactions in real-time, hence enabling proactive interventions by institutions before cases of compliance escalate. Going further, RegTech ensures real-time monitoring of changes in the regulatory environment, which consequently keeps the organization abreast of the changes in requirements that could occur. This would save the organization from expensive penalties and reputational damage. It also enhances operational efficiency as well as supports a culture of transparency and accountability among the firms within the finance sector. Going forward, the increasingly demanding and complex nature of the regulatory landscape will mean RegTech solutions with a basis in machine learning are going to be necessities for firms wanting to effectively navigate such issues and move forward toward successful improvements in compliance and reduced operational risks and regained customer trust.

Scalable Insights

Scalable insights powered by machine learning can now answer the challenges and opportunities pertaining to exponential growth in the data-driven landscape of today's finance. As financial institutions deal with mass and continually increasing datasets, the scalability through which machine learning algorithms will have to process all such information to make it ready in time for proper actionable insights can really power strategic decision-making. These scalable tools can analyze complex data streams with great speed, thus enabling firms to determine the greater patterns and trends about anything related to risk management, investment strategies, and customer service with unprecedented speed and accuracy. For example, in risk management, it can analyze historical data and real-time inputs to identify emerging threats or opportunities in advance and proactively take measures to mitigate potential losses. In investment strategies, algorithmic analysis can evaluate several factors, such as market conditions and macroeconomic indicators, and will assist portfolio managers in better optimizing their asset allocations and improving returns. Again, customer service will enhance personalization efforts where the machine learning model tracks customer interactions and preferences so the institutions provide their offerings and enhance client satisfaction. Data volumes will only expand in financial markets [27], and yet the change in markets calls for new ways of capitalizing on scalable insights through machine learning to remain competitive as well as better address the changed needs of these stakeholders.

Collaborative Intelligence

Collaborative intelligence is this transformational technology located at the intersection of human intuition and machine learning capability to unlock new opportunities in the financial sector. Advanced machine learning models can help foster better quality decision-making processes with fundamental quantitative insights that are merged with qualitative judgment, especially in portfolio management and investment strategy. For example, while a human portfolio manager is seasoned in the business and intimately aware of market dynamics, machine learning algorithms can process petabytes of data to identify trends, correlations, and anomalies that may not be immediately obvious. This synergy will allow professionals to make more informed investment decisions while combining qualitative insights with quantitative data analysis for a well-rounded view of markets. Additional benefits from machine learning models exist and can learned and adapted with time while at the same time feeding real-time feedback to human judgment. Essentially, therefore, financial institutions can improve their processes in risk assessment by using improvements to portfolio performance and innovation after leveraging the best of human judgment and machine intelligence. This collaborative approach not only leads to a more agile and responsive financial environment but enables organizations to better face complex challenges to result in improved outcomes for investors and stakeholders [17].

CONCLUSION

Machine learning is becoming indispensable in financial analytics, transforming the way institutions analyze data, manage risk, and make decisions. As financial data continues to grow in volume and complexity, machine learning offers significant opportunities to extract meaningful insights and gain a competitive advantage. However, addressing the challenges—such as data quality, non-stationarity, and model interpretability—will be critical to unlocking the full potential of machine learning in finance.

REFERENCES

[1]   J. Sen, R. Sen, and A. Dutta, "Introductory chapter: Machine learning in finance—emerging trends and challenges," *In: Machine Learning – Algorithms, Models and Applications*, pg 1, 2022.

[2]   S. Kumar, D. Sharma, S. Rao, W.M. Lim, and S.K. Mangla, "Past, present, and future of sustainable finance: insights from big data analytics through machine learning of scholarly research", *Ann. Oper.*

Res., pp. 1-44, 2022.
[PMID: 35002001]

[3]   Y. Chen, K.C. Cheung, K. Fan, and P. Yam, *Financial data analytics with machine learning, optimization and statistics.* John Wiley & Sons, 2024.

[4]   R. Shekhar, D. S. Tomar, R. K. Pateriya, and B. Sharan, "Human activity recognition with smartphone using classical machine learning models," In: *Proc. 10th Int. Conf. on Computing for Sustainable Global Development (INDIACom)*, pp. 85–90, 2023.

[5]   R. Hassan, B. Sharan, N. Kumari, T. Rafiq, G. Thakur, and R. Bhargav, "Prediction of chronic diseases using machine learning classifiers", *In 2023 10th Int. Conf. comput. Sustain. Glob. Dev. (INDIACom)*, pp. 885-889, 2023.

[6]   H. Wasserbacher, and M. Spindler, "Machine learning for financial forecasting, planning and analysis: recent developments and pitfalls", *Digit. Finance,* vol. 4, no. 1, pp. 63-88, 2022.
[http://dx.doi.org/10.1007/s42521-021-00046-2]

[7]   M. Faheem, M.U.H.A.M.M.A.D. Aslam, and S.R.I.D.E.V.I. Kakolu, "Enhancing financial forecasting accuracy through AI-driven predictive analytics models", *Retrieved,* no. December, p. 11, 2024.

[8]   R. Shekhar, D.S. Tomar, B. Sharan, and R.K. Pateriya, "Human activity recognition using deep learning techniques for healthcare applications". *In 2024 15th nternational conference on computing communication and networking technologies (ICCCNT)*, pp. 1-6, 2024.
[http://dx.doi.org/10.1109/ICCCNT61001.2024.10725736]

[9]   B. Sharan, M. Husain, M.N. Ahmed, A.K. Sagar, A. Ali, A.T. Siddiqui, and M.R. Hussain, "Numerical, machine learning and deep-learning based framework for weather prediction", *Int. J. Comput. Sci. Netw. Secur.*, vol. 24, no. 9, pp. 63-76, 2024.

[10]   M. Ajagalla, M. Pandey, J. Choudhary, and L. Kumar, "Root vegetable crop recommendation system based on soil properties and environmental factors", *International Conference on Data Science, Machine Learning and Applications*, pp. 86-98, 2023.Singapore

[11]   M. Chhabra, B. Sharan, M. Elbarachi, and M. Kumar, "Intelligent waste classification approach based on improved multi-layered convolutional neural network", *Multimedia Tools Appl.,* vol. 83, no. 36, pp. 84095-84120, 2024.
[http://dx.doi.org/10.1007/s11042-024-18939-w]

[12]   M. Panchal, B. Sharan, and P. Dwivedi, "Comprehensive analysis of machine learning approaches for breast cancer detection and classification", *In 2023 10th Int. Conf. Comput. Sustain. Glob. Dev. (INDIACom)*, IEEE, pp. 867-872, 2023.

[13]   M.F. Dixon, I. Halperin, and P. Bilokon, *Machine learning in finance.* vol. 1170. Springer International Publishing: New York, NY, USA, 2020.
[http://dx.doi.org/10.1007/978-3-030-41068-1]

[14]   M. L. D. Prado, *Advances in financial machine learning.* John Wiley & Sons, 2018.

[15]   O.A. Bello, "Machine learning algorithms for credit risk assessment: an economic and financial analysis", *Int. J. Manag.*, vol. 10, no. 1, pp. 109-133, 2023.

[16]   A. Singla, and H. Jangir, "A comparative approach to predictive analytics with machine learning for fraud detection of realtime financial data", *2020 International Conference on Emerging Trends in Communication, Control and Computing (ICONC3)*, IEEE., pp. 1-4, 2020.
[http://dx.doi.org/10.1109/ICONC345789.2020.9117435]

[17]   T. Damrongsakmethee, and V.E. Neagoe, "Data mining and machine learning for financial analysis", *Indian J. Sci. Technol.*, vol. 10, no. 39, pp. 1-7, 2017.
[http://dx.doi.org/10.17485/ijst/2017/v10i39/119861]

[18]   P. Sarlin and J. Mezei, "Introduction to the minitrack on machine learning and predictive analytics in accounting, finance, and management," In: *Proc. Hawaii Int. Conf. on System Sciences (HICSS)*, 2021.

[19]   K. Oroy and P. Evan, *Machine Learning Applications in Finance: Predictive Analytics and Risk Management*, EasyChair, no. 12239, 2024.

[20]   S. Aziz and M. Dowling, "Machine learning and AI for risk management," In: *Disrupting Finance: FinTech Strategy in the 21st Century*, pp. 33–50, 2019.
[http://dx.doi.org/10.1007/978-3-030-02330-0_3]

[21]   J.W. Goodell, S. Kumar, W.M. Lim, and D. Pattnaik, "Artificial intelligence and machine learning in finance: Identifying foundations, themes, and research clusters from bibliometric analysis", *J. Behav. Exp. Finance,* vol. 32, p. 100577, 2021.
[http://dx.doi.org/10.1016/j.jbef.2021.100577]

[22]   K. Kaur, Y. Kumar, and S. Kaur, "Artificial intelligence and machine learning in financial services to improve the business system", In: *Comput. Intell. Mod. Bus. Syst.: Emerg. Appl. Strateg.* Springer Nature Singapore: Singapore, 2023, pp. 3-30.

[23]   L. S. Guryanova, and N. A. Roman Yatsenko, "Machine learning methods and models, predictive analytics and applications",

[24]   Schmitt, Marc, Artificial intelligence in business analytics: capturing value with machine learning applications in financial services. 2020,
[http://dx.doi.org/10.48730/5s00-jd45]

[25]   S. Singla, *Machine Learning for Finance: Beginner's guide to explore machine learning in banking and finance.* English Edition, 2021.

[26]   M. Paramesha, N. Rane, and J. Rane, "Artificial intelligence, machine learning, deep learning, and blockchain in financial and banking services: a comprehensive review", *SSRN,* vol. 1, no. 2, pp. 51-67, 2024.
[http://dx.doi.org/10.2139/ssrn.4855893]

[27]   Bryan Kelly, and Dacheng Xiu, "Financial machine learning", *Foundations and Trends® in Finance,* vol. 13, no. 3-4, pp. 205-363, 2023.
[http://dx.doi.org/10.3386/w31502]

CHAPTER 2

Attention Inspired Human Activity Recognition Models Using Deep Learning: A Review

A. Aminu[1], Rajneesh Kumar Singh[1,*], Gaurav Kumar[2], Arun Prakash Agarwal[3] and S. Pratap Singh[4]

[1] *Sharda School of Engineering & Technology, Sharda University, Greater Noida, Uttar Pradesh, India*

[2] *Department of Computer Science and Application, School of Computer Science and Engineering, IILM University, Greater Noida, India*

[3] *School of Computer Science Engineering & Technology, Bennett University, Greater Noida, Uttar Pradesh, India*

[4] *Thapar Institute of Engineering and Technology, Patiala, Punjab, India*

Abstract: Human Activity Recognition (HAR) plays a critical role in segregating and distinguishing human actions among data generated from videos and other numerous sensing modalities, such as accelerometer, gyroscope, GPS, and magnetometer. HAR is considered a rapidly growing field that has revolutionized numerous areas, such as healthcare, manufacturing, security, smart homes, *etc.* Manual extraction of features in traditional machine learning approaches makes it difficult to handle the spatial and temporal complexities of real-world datasets, thereby necessitating the need for Deep Learning algorithms that offer automatic feature extraction to effectively capture both the spatial and temporal data. This chapter provides a review of Deep Learning models for HAR, focusing on advancements in CNN and LSTM and their variant architectures that play a significant role in handling complex and multivariate datasets gathered from wearable devices and smartphones. Furthermore, attention mechanisms, such as the self-attention and squeeze and excitation modules, have significantly enhanced model performance by focusing on relevant feature maps and recalibrating them adaptively. These mechanisms do not only improve the accuracy but also the interpretability of the model by concentrating on the important aspects of the data in consideration. This chapter also highlights hybrid models that combine CNN and LSTM and their variants for more accurate HAR, especially when working with sensor-based datasets. Additionally, it also examines that incorporation of attention mechanisms not only boosts accuracy but also optimizes the complexity of the models. Key trends in attention-driven deep learning methods are examined, indicating their growing importance in real-world human activity recognition applications.

---

[*] **Corresponding author Rajneesh Kumar Singh:** Sharda School of Engineering & Technology, Sharda University, Greater Noida, Uttar Pradesh, India; Tel: +91 82853 97615;
E-mail: rajneesh.kumar@sharda.edu.in

Ashwani Kumar, Mohit Kumar, Avinash Kumar Sharma & Yojna Arora (Eds.)
All rights reserved-© 2025 Bentham Science Publishers

Keywords: Artificial intelligence (AI), Deep learning (ML), Human activity, Wearable sensor.

INTRODUCTION

Many algorithms within the field of artificial intelligence have been developed to effectively categorize and classify human actions. Several Deep Learning models have been widely used to achieve better accuracy in comparison to other traditional approaches based on Machine Learning. Moreover, the attention mechanism by Deep Learning approaches significantly boosts the performance of a model [1].

Singh *et al*. [2] introduced an effective and highly regarded technique of incorporating a self-attention mechanism that effectively extracts and analyzes the sequential patterns from time series data using some stacked layers of the LSTM model. The major advantage of attention-based models is to enhance the model's accuracy and complexity by concentrating on identifying the most relevant features from the dataset under consideration. This study provides a review of deep learning models for human activity while incorporating attention mechanisms. It explores recent advances in deep learning models for human activity recognition, as well as the approaches proposed for the hybrid amalgamation of several deep and machine-learning algorithms. Moreover, it discusses published articles within the domain, focusing on their key findings. In addition to that, a summary of the deep learning models that incorporate attention mechanisms is also presented.

Human Activity

Human activity includes any motions, signs, and physical acts that necessitate using energy, such as walking, running, jogging, eating, drinking, *etc* [3]. In a broader term, human activity can be categorized into simple and complex activities. Simple human actions take posture and body movement into consideration while performing different tasks. Such activities include running, jogging, walking, *etc*, while the other category (complex) includes carrying out simpler ones in conjunction with other activities. These include subjects brushing their teeth and, at the same time, performing a simple activity like standing or sitting. By utilizing deep learning techniques on sensor data collected from different sensing modalities, various human activities, ranging from simple to complex, will be classified into sub-categories, such as ambulation-related, general hand-oriented, and hand-oriented activities related to eating, as illustrated in Fig. (**1**). Sensor-based systems can be further classified into ambient, device-bound (object-tagged), and wearable [4].

Ambulation Oriented Activities	
1. Walking	4. Stairs
2. Standing	5. Jogging
3. Kicking	6. Sitting

Hand Oriented Activities(General)	
7. Writing	10. Typing
8. Brushing Teeth	11. Clapping
9. Folding Clothes	12. Dribbling
13. Playing Catch	

Hand Oriented Activities (Eating)	
14. Eating Sandwich	16. Drinking
15. Eating Chips	17. Eating Pasta
18. Eating Soup	

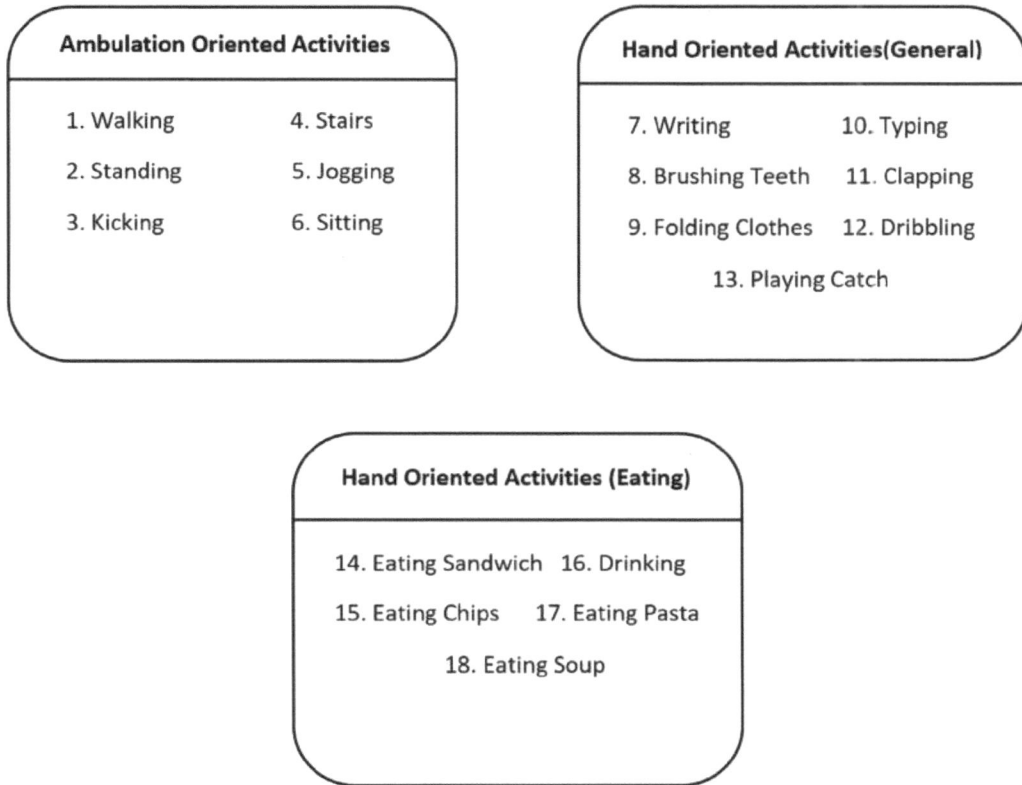

Fig. (1). Categories of human activities [3].

Generally, two approaches are broadly categorized for human activity recognition systems in terms of data gathering and accumulation, namely vision-based and sensor-based, as shown in Fig. (**2**).

Vision-based systems employ optical sensors or video surveillance cameras to detect and interpret different activities of individuals being studied. A significant challenge of these systems is the privacy of the subjects, as it may not be feasible to install cameras in every location due to ethical regulations [5]. Moreover, vision-based Human Activity Recognition (HAR) relies heavily on graphical activities, which necessitate substantial computing power. Vision-based HAR is classified into two modules: motion-based approach and video-based systems. The motion-based approach utilizes a wearable marker Motion Capture (MoCap) system, which is known for its accuracy in tracking complex human movements. However, this method has drawbacks, such as the requirement for multiple camera setups and the need for sensors to be affixed to the body. On the other hand, video-based systems utilize depth video cameras and do not require markers, making them increasingly popular for everyday applications due to the ease of deployment. Park *et al.* [6] demonstrated the effectiveness of data from depth vision cameras in HAR by extracting features from human actions and applying traditional classifiers like Hidden Markov Model (HMM) and Conditional Random Fields.

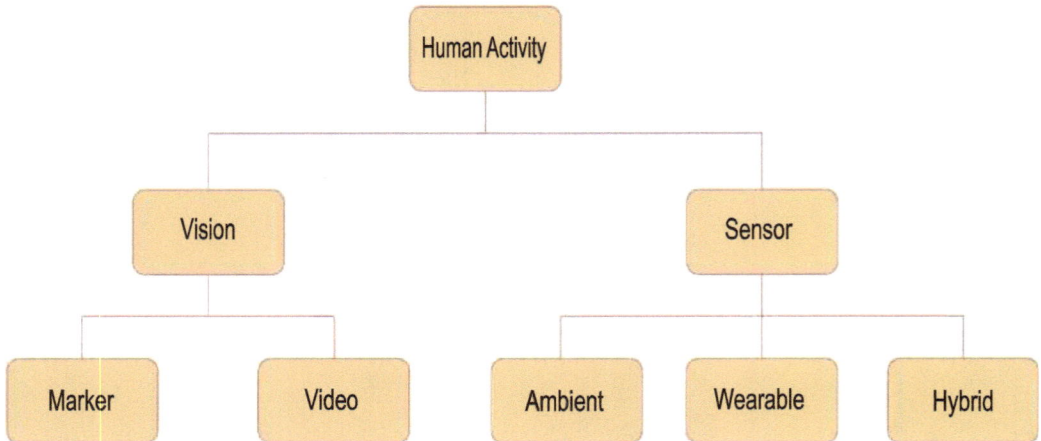

Fig. (2). Human activities modalities.

Sensor-based approaches, on the other hand, aim to discover patterns in daily human activities using wearable or embedded sensors. They are critical components of many practical applications in urban planning, smart homes, and personal healthcare. Many categories of sensor-based systems are proposed depending on the mode of usage.

Ambient sensors provide potential information about activities performed in smart home situations due to their capacity to protect user's privacy and other issues.

Wearable sensors, also known as body sensors, are becoming popular because they are very cheap and use low power. Wearable sensors have become a centre of interest in research and development. These electronic sensors can be worn on the human body. They are often used to collect and detect physical data about the person, such as body part motions, and to identify basic activities.

Hybrid sensors involve the use of multiple heterogenous sources to accumulate sensor readings, which can significantly assist in research in HAR and support the development of applications like commercial smart home systems.

Machine Learning Methods used Recognition of Human Activities

Machine learning models are designed to create systems that can autonomously learn from data, uncover hidden patterns, and make informed decisions with minimal human involvement. Thus, Machine Learning can be best defined according to Mitchell and Mitchell [6] as: "a computer program is said to learn from experience E with respect to some task T and some performance measure P, if its performance on T, as measured by P, improves with experience E." ML models are widely categorized into supervised and unsupervised models that predict outcomes from labeled and unlabeled data, respectively.

Supervised machine learning algorithms are further segregated into two main types of problems: classification and regression problems.

Classification involves developing a model or function that allows for the categorization of data into distinct groups or classes based on specific characteristics or features. In the process of classification, input parameters are used to group data under various labels before predictions are made about the labels for the data themselves. Examples of supervised learning algorithms used for classification are Naive Bayes, K-Nearest Neighbours, *etc*.

Regression is the process of establishing a model or function for discrete values or classes to be used in place of continuous real values for data differentiation. In addition, based on past data, it can determine the distribution movement. Regression predictive models forecast quantities; hence, their accuracy must be expressed as an error in the predictions made by the model.

Traditional machine learning models have been effectively applied to categorize human actions from data generated by different sensor modalities. Several successful attempts have been made to automatically utilize machine learning algorithms to classify and categorize human actions in healthcare and security surveillance. A few of them are summarized in Table **1**.

Table 1. Summary of machine learning-based models.

Authors	Algorithm	Description	Advantages
Ehatisham-Ul-Haq *et al.* [7]	KNN and SVM	The model utilized data from multiple modalities, which are a combination of depth-sensing cameras and wearable motion-tracking sensors.	The result indicated that the model provides the overall best accuracy of 97.2%.

(Table 1) cont.....

Authors	Algorithm	Description	Advantages
Ahmed *et al.* [8]	SVM	It utilized feature selection hybridized by employing wrapper and filter methods for smart-watch sensor data using the SVM to test and identify human activities.	The model achieved the highest accuracy of 96.8%, which was 8% higher than without using feature selection.
Randhawa *et al.* [9]	KNN, Decision Tree, and SVM	Three machine learning algorithms were compared to accurately classify physical activities between normal and violent attacks from a fabric sensor attached to a worn jacket.	The result indicated that SVM outperformed the rest with an accuracy of 98.8%.
Subasi [10]	Naïve Bayes, KNN, SVM, RF, CART, C4.5, REPTree, LADTree	A comparative study was performed among three machine learning algorithms on data generated from a dual (smartphone and wearable sensor) sensing modality.	SVM outperformed the other algorithms with an overall best accuracy of 99.43%
Logacjov *et al.* [11]	BiLSTM, XGB, CNN and conventional MLs (SVM, KNN, and RF)	Seven machine learning models were employed to assess a dataset that was professionally annotated and collected in an uncontrolled environment, where individuals wore dual accelerometers.	Although all the algorithms achieved a high-performance measure, SVM outperformed the rest with a better accuracy and precision rate.
Garcia-Gonzalez *et al.* [12]	Support Vector Machine (SVM), Decision Tree, Multilayer Perceptron (MLP), Naïve Bayes, K-Nearest Neighbors (KNN), Random Forest, and XGBoost (XGB)	A real-life dataset that was obtained in an uncontrolled environment was utilized, and various algorithms were utilized to classify activities from such datasets.	Random Forest outperformed the other algorithms with an accuracy of 92.79%.
Moin *et al.* [14]	Hyperdimensional (HD) computing	A biosensing system for surface electromyography has been created that employs advanced computing techniques to process and classify hand gestures, enabling real-time updates and inference of the model.	The system can effectively classify 21 hand gesture activities with an accuracy of 92.87%.

Ehatisham-Ul-Haq *et al.* [7] suggested a reliable strategy for feature-level fusion across multiple modalities to strengthen human action recognition performance. It addressed the problem when using the camera-based and sensor-based modality.

However, It operated using actions that had already been segmented and were not applicable in practice. In multiview human activity recognition (HAR), the person's orientation relative to the camera remains consistent during the action being recognized.

Ahmed *et al.* [8] suggested a hybrid approach for feature selection that combines both wrapper and filter methods. It utilized a sequential floating forward search (SFFS) for accurate feature extraction and then fed them to multiclass SVM for classification tasks. The experimental research outcomes demonstrated that the SVM outscored with an accuracy of 96.81%, approximately 8% higher than the performance without feature selection.

Randhawa *et al.* [9] introduced an innovative method for distinguishing between normal activities and violent assaults using data collected from a fabric sensor system. This system, which included fabric pressure and stretch sensors as well as a 9-degree-of-freedom accelerometer, was embedded in a jacket worn by participants. Three different machine learning classifiers, namely K-Nearest Neighbors (KNN), Decision Tree, and Support Vector Machine (SVM), were implemented. Among these, the SVM classifier yielded the highest accuracy, achieving a remarkable 98.8%. However, it is worth noting that the research took place in a controlled environment, which may have limited the participants' ability to engage in more natural movements.

Subasi *et al.* [10] conducted experiments with various techniques to handle activities generated from dual sensing modalities in smartphones and body-worn sensors. A comparative study was carried out between machine learning algorithms (Naïve Bayes, KNN, SVM, RF, CART, C4.5, REPTree, and LADTree), among which SVM outperformed the rest with an accuracy of 99.43%. However, it was observed that body-worn sensors provide more accuracy than smartphone sensors.

Logacjov *et al.* [11] proposed a dataset that was carefully annotated and collected in a natural environment, where participants wore dual accelerometers, one placed on their back and the other on their thigh, to gather data. The study analysed the dataset on seven baseline algorithms. It has been observed that with respect to the dataset, some labels can be well predicted while others cannot, this is due to similarities and ambiguity between some activities. The models struggled to effectively address the issue of class imbalance, making it challenging to achieve accurate human activity recognition in real-world, uncontrolled conditions.

Garcia-Gonzalez *et al.* [12] carried out experiments on a dataset collected using a smartphone sensor in a laboratory-free environment, which provides users with the freedom to place the smartphone in any position within the body. The accuracy of the best-performing model (Random Forest) across all configurations of feature sets and window sizes within the dataset was found to be significantly higher than the previously reported, improving from 74.39% to 92.97%. However, no significant differences between different window sizes were observed. Thus, any choice would be feasible depending on the problem in consideration.

Hayat *et al*. [13] created an autonomous activity monitoring system that employed various machine and deep learning techniques (RF, k-NN, SVM, ANN, and LSTM) to automatically detect the activities of old persons. The LSTM approach produced the best accuracy of 95.05% out of all the techniques, which is noteworthy because it is difficult to create a precise HAR system due to the wide variety of activities, some of which are quite similar to one another. However, the model can be improved by testing with more extensive datasets and a greater variety of activities.

Moin *et al*. [14] introduced a fully autonomous wearable Surface Electro-Myography (sEMG) biosensing system that employs high-definition computing for the processing and classification of hand gestures. In contrast to other advanced gesture recognition systems, the proposed system was found to be capable of performing model updates, inference, and training locally and in real-time, enabling it to adapt to constantly changing contextual conditions.

Deep Learning-Based Approaches for Human Activity Recognition

Many approaches have been utilized to categorize human activities automatically using deep learning algorithms. However, some tradeoffs and overlapping priorities are a great concern in declaring the best-performing approach. Fig. (**3**) depicts the categories of deep learning-based models and their hybrid combinations that are utilized for human activity recognition.

Wan *et al*. [15] analyzed the performance of some algorithms (CNN, LSTM, BLSTM, MLP, and SVM) to classify human activities using smartphone datasets. A comparative study was carried out to determine the best-performing algorithm among others. An experiment was also conducted separately for each of the mentioned algorithms using UCI and Pampa2 datasets. Since SVM is considered one of the best among machine learning algorithms, it has been outperformed by deep learning models. The structure of the algorithms should be optimized to give better performance measures. However, for further validation, these algorithms should be tested on larger datasets that contain complex human activities.

Qin *et al*. [16] proposed a novel technique that combines global and local-time series features to encode time-series into GAF images. Standard convolutional neural networks (CNNs) commonly used for image recognition can then be applied to train models using this new representation. In order to confirm that imaging time series is feasible, the proposed model was validated by conducting a variety of tests. Additionally, the proposed model employed a fusion of ResNet to solve the problem of heterogeneity of data. The model achieved the best accuracy on smaller datasets. However, this approach needs to be tested and validated on larger datasets to make perfect generalizations.

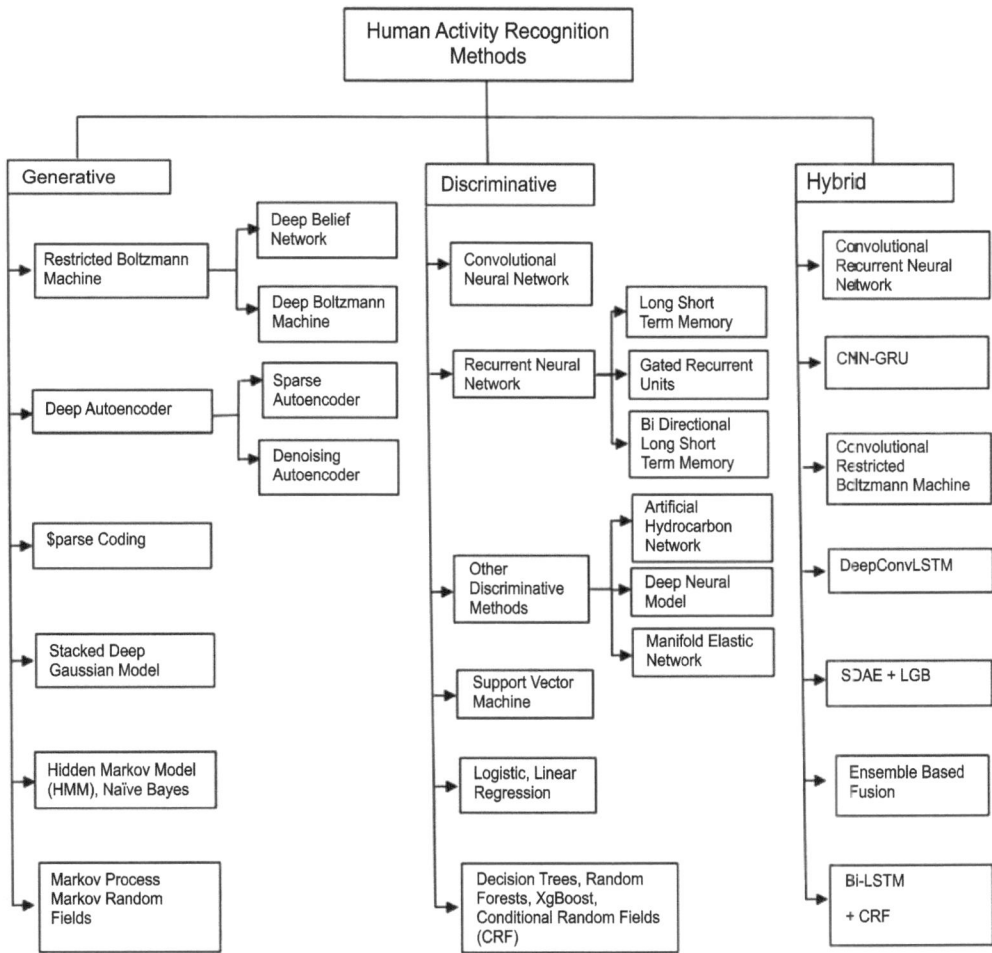

Fig. (3). Deep learning models for human activity recognition.

Mekruksavanich and Jitpattanakul [17] developed four LSTM models to investigate how well they recognize human activities by utilizing several smartphone sensors, such as the tri-axial gyroscope and accelerometer. Vanilla LSTM, 2-stacked, and 3-stacked LSTM-based networks were applied to categorize publicly available datasets with 10-fold cross-validation techniques precisely. A hybrid 4-layer CNN-LSTM network was also proposed to improve accuracy, which indicated a performance increase of about 2.24%. The generalization of the model needs to be improved by evaluating it on more complex activities.

Hybrid Deep Learning-Based Models

Models that include multiple deep learning models are referred to as hybrid models, such as CNNs and RNNs (Table 2). Such algorithms help detect the spatial and temporal features when extracted. Therefore, combining CNNs with RNNs could lead to improved performance when it comes to identifying activities that are composed of different signal distributions and time periods. CNNs using Stacked Autoencoders (SAEs) and RBM have been employed in other investigations. In these investigations, the generative models expedited the training phase while CNN handled feature extraction [18].

Table 2. Summary of hybrid deep learning-based models.

Authors	Algorithm	Description	Advantages
Xia *et al.* [19]	LSTM, CNN	In this model, CNN was stacked on top of LSTM, followed by Global Average Pooling (GAP) layer. The model was tested and evaluated on WISDM, UCI-HAR, and OPPORTUNITY datasets.	It solves the problem of long convergence duration while achieving the highest accuracy compared to the baseline algorithms.
Nafea *et al.* [18]	CNN-BiLSTM	An end-to-end convolutional neural network with different kernel sizes combined with a bidirectional LSTM to capture multi-resolution features.	The model achieved the highest accuracy of 98.53% and 97.05% with WISDM and UCI-HAR, respectively.
Dua *et al.* [21]	CNN-GRU	It utilized multiple CNN inputs and a GRU for feature extraction and handling long-term dependencies, respectively. It was experimented on UCI-HAR, WISDM, and PAMAP2 conventional datasets.	The model is efficient with GRU compared to using its LSTM variants.
Gupta [3]	CNN-GRU	It utilized CNN and GRU in identifying complex human action from the WISDM dataset using the sliding window segmentation method and AutoML as baseline models.	It achieved the best accuracy of 96.54% relative to the state-of-the-art techniques in the field, such as Inception Time and DeepConvLSTM, with an accuracy of 95.79% and 87.65%, respectively.

(Table 2) cont.....

Authors	Algorithm	Description	Advantages
Khan *et al.* [20]	CNN-LSTM	It combined the hybrid fusion of CNN and LSTM on a new dataset that provided 12 home-based physical activities from 20 participants.	The mode: achieved the overall best accuracy of 90.89% on 30 frames in comparison to other deep-learning approaches.
Challa *et al.* [22]	CNN-BiLSTM	Different combinations of CNN filter dimensions were used to capture local, spatial, and temporal dependencies to improve the feature extraction process and recognition accuracy.	The model achieved overall best accuracy of 96.05%, 96.37%, and 94.29% on WISDM, UCI-HAR, and PAMAP2 datasets, respectively.
Garcia-Gonzalez *et al.* [23]	Depthwise separable CNN with LSTM and depthwise separable CNN with bidirectional LSTM	Separable CNNs were hybridized with LSTM and its variants to categorize real-life datasets collected from participants in a free-living environment.	It achieved a peak accuracy of 94.8%.

Xia *et al.* [19] proposed a model that combined the capabilities of LSTM and CNN algorithms to classify human activities using sensor data. It aimed to address the problem of long convergence times and achieve a generalized result by evaluating the model's performance on three public datasets (WISDM, UCI-HAR, and OPPORTUNITY). The proposed model consists of a stacked CNN on top of an eight-layer LSTM. The pre-processed data is first fed into the two LSTM layers of 64 neurons combined, followed by two convolutional layers that have max pooling layers in between. The Global Average Pooling (GAP) layer is applied in the model, with batch normalization incorporated before the output layer, which consists of a dense layer and SoftMax activation.

Nafea *et al.* [18], an end-to-end convolutional neural network featuring a variable kernel combined with bi-directional long short-term memory (BiLSTM), was introduced to effectively capture features across different resolutions. After extensive testing, it was determined that the CNN-BiLSTM architecture effectively extracted both spatial and temporal data. The proposed model maintained the relationship between movement and spatial variables. In order to develop a targeted approach for the specific application, various factors must be considered, leading to the selection of an appropriate strategy. Consequently, despite the existence of several distinct methodologies, there remain unresolved issues that require further exploration.

Khan *et al.* [20] suggested a hybrid fusion of CNN stacked on top of LSTM to provide an indoor activity recognition system to effectively identify various activities aimed at enhancing a person's physical and emotional well-being. The hybrid model performed exceptionally well (achieving 90.89% accuracy) in terms of activity identification for single-person tasks, but it might not be able to handle multiple people's activities with more efficiency.

Dua *et al.* [21] introduced a multiple-headed CNN combined with a Gated Recurrent Unit (GRU), a variant of LSTM, to leverage the powerful feature extraction capabilities of CNNs along with the sequential modeling strengths of GRUs for classifying time-series data. The multi-input architecture improved the model's capacity to recognize features at various depths, from simple to complex, leading to more precise activity predictions. The incorporation of GRU layers allowed the model to effectively learn long-term dependencies in sequential data, whereas convolutional layers were particularly skilled at identifying local patterns. Experimental results from the UCI-HAR, WISDM, and PAMAP2 datasets revealed that the proposed model outperformed several existing methods for HAR. Furthermore, the findings indicated that the multi-input CNN-GRU model surpassed its multi-input CNN-LSTM counterpart.

Gupta [3] also presented CNN-GRU, which is a hybrid fusion DL model for identifying intricate human actions. It utilizes unprocessed sensor data from the WISDM dataset, which includes data collected from smartphones and smartwatches. A sliding window segmentation method is utilized, and AutoML is used to generate baseline models like DeepConvL-STM and InceptionTime. Findings indicated that smartwatches are more accurate than smartphones in identifying composite human activities. Moreover, hybrid deep learning models demonstrated superior capability in autonomously capturing spatial and temporal features from raw sensor data for classifying complex activities, compared to the other deep learning models examined, which utilized more intricate architectures. This leads to improved performance metrics. It is also suggested that deep transformer models should be adopted to handle time series classification.

To address the shortcomings encountered in LSTM-based models, Challa *et al.* [22] proposed a Multibranch CNN-BiLSTM model that requires little pre-processing to function directly on raw data obtained from wearable sensors. This model leverages the advantages of CNNs and BiLSTMs, enabling it to capture both short-term and long-term dependencies in sequential data. The proposed multibranch CNN-BiLSTM model appears to have good cross-dataset generalization.

Most of the activities considered in past literature were monitored in a laboratory-controlled environment. Two main issues affect the performance evaluation of a model when experiments are conducted on such data: first, the activities do not transfer easily to the real-life domain, and second, inconsistent device positioning during experiments can introduce variability. Garcia-Gonzalez *et al.* [23] utilized the most appropriate configuration of CNN-LSTM to categorize human activities from the real-life dataset that was collected in an uncontrolled environment. Hybrid implementations of DS-CNN-LSTM and DS-CNN-Bi-LSTM models were carried out using Depthwise Separable Convolutional Neural Networks (DS-CNN) combined with either a Long Short-Term Memory (LSTM) or a Bidirectional Long Short-Term Memory (Bi-LSTM) layer in such a way that the model's spatial features were extracted by CNN, which was further enhanced by LSTM.

Attention Mechanism-Based Deep Learning Models for Human Activity Recognition

The majority of current deep learning models heavily influence feature distinction determination during the parameter training phase by assigning equal weight to disparate visual and temporal signals. However, utilizing an attention mechanism can significantly enhance the performance of deep learning models by focusing on relevant features, improving contextual understanding, and enabling better handling of long sequences. Table **3** presents a summary of a few deep learning-based approaches incorporating attention mechanisms in classifying human action recognition.

Table 3. Attention-based human activity recognition.

Authors	Algorithm	Description	Advantages
Dai *et al.* [24]	CLSTM with attention	It utilized LSTM and CLSTM streams to encode temporal spatial-temporal features. An experiment was carried out on datasets, namely HMDB51, UCF101, and JHMDB.	The model achieved a higher accuracy of 96.9% when applied to the UCF11 sports dataset, which was relatively higher than other models.
Singh *et al.* [2]	CNN and LSTM	It utilized ConvLSTM with a self-attention mechanism with varying filters of CNN (1,2,3,6,12) and LSTM units (8,16,32,64) and self-attention length (8,16,32,64). An experiment was implemented on MHEALTH, USC-HAD, UTD-MHAD, WHARF, and WISDM datasets.	The model achieved the highest accuracy of 94.86% using the MHEALTH dataset compared to baseline ConvLSTM, which achieved 93.80%.

(Table 3) cont.....

Authors	Algorithm	Description	Advantages
Muhammad *et al.* [25]	DCNN and BiLSTM	It utilized a DCNN To capture and extract key discriminative features, which were subsequently provided to the BiLSTM for evaluation on UCF11, UCF sports, and J-HMDB datasets.	It achieved an accuracy of 98.3%, 99.1%, and 80.2% for the respective datasets.
Zanobya and Jamil [26]	CNN	A multiheaded CNN induced with squeeze and excitation module as attention WISDM and UCI HAR.	The attention-induced models outperformed the non-attention and other established algorithms, achieving an accuracy of 98.18% and 95.38% using WISDM and UCI-HAR datasets, respectively.
Mekruksavanich and Jitpattanakul [28]	ResNet and BiGRU	It embedded squeeze and excitation modules as an attention mechanism to a ResNet-BiGRU model and experimented using WISDM, IM-WSHA, and UCI-HAR.	The resultant model achieved a better accuracy of 99.39%, *i.e.*, 2.4% ahead of the state-of-the-art approaches.
Gao *et al.* [29]	Dual Attention Network (DanHAR) using residual CNN with channel and temporal attention mechanisms.	A dual attention mechanism model was proposed, focusing on both channel and temporal aspects of multimodal sensor data to enhance activity recognition accuracy on WISDM, UNIMIB SHAR, PAMAP2, and Opportunity.	Improved accuracy across datasets, with relative improvements of up to 5% over traditional CNNs.
Buffelli and Vandin [30]	Attention-based deep learning framework (TrASenD) with transfer learning for personalization.	A purely attention-based model for human activity recognition (HAR) replaced recurrent neural networks (RNNs) and utilized transfer learning for personalization, enhancing long-sequence processing and user adaptation. It was tested on the Opportunity, PAMAP2, and WISDM datasets.	TrASenD was evaluated on three datasets, demonstrating a 7% enhancement compared to the leading models in the field.

Authors	Algorithm	Description	Advantages
Laitrakun [31]	Merging-Squeeze-Excitation (MSE) feature fusion using CNN with AlexNet, LeNet5, and VGG16.	The MSE feature fusion method was introduced to improve human activity recognition (HAR) by recalibrating feature maps during the fusion process to prioritize relevant information, resulting in enhanced classification performance on the PAMAP2, DaLiAc, and DSAD datasets.	The recognition rates achieved for the datasets are as follows: PAMAP2 at 99.24%, DaLiAc at 98.59%, and DSAD at 98.04%, surpassing the performance of state-of-the-art models.
Akter *et al.* [32]	Attention-based CNN model with CBAM modules (AM-DLFC).	A lightweight deep learning model incorporating attention mechanisms integrated feature maps from various stages to enhance classification accuracy on the KU-HAR, UCI-HAR, and WISDM datasets.	The model attained accuracies of 96.86% on KU-HAR, 93.48% on UCI-HAR, and 93.89% on WISDM.

Dai *et al.* [24] proposed an end-to-end, two-stream attention-based LSTM model, incorporating both temporal and spatial-temporal features, driven by a visual attention mechanism to improve human action recognition in videos. The model can give varying degrees of attention to the outputs of each deep feature map and selectively concentrate on the features that work well for the original input images. The attention mechanism's ability to adaptively learn intricate spatial and temporal attention features improves action identification at every stage of long short-term memory. The results indicate that this approach performs better than similar deep learning models and is better suited to shifting settings.

Singh *et al.* [2] utilized data generated from multiple wearable sensors for effective action recognition. Deep learning architectures were used to capture the spatial and temporal features using attention mechanisms in identifying embedding when decoding actions. The embeddings of data generated by CNN and LSTM were used by the self-attention layer to generate feature representations. The model was evaluated against baseline algorithms (CNN and LSTM) and other state-of-the-art methods, and better recognition accuracy was found. The model could be improved by providing an extension on different mechanisms that include global and local attention in comparison with the performance of the self-attention mechanism.

Muhammad *et al.* [25] suggested an attention mechanism based on a dilated Bi-directional LSTM (BiLSTM) in conjunction with a Dilated Convolutional Neural

Network (DCNN). This approach emphasizes the most relevant features in the input frame to effectively recognize different human actions in videos. The DCNN employs residual blocks to extract prominent discriminative features, which are subsequently input into a BiLSTM to capture long-term dependencies. This process is enhanced by incorporating an attention mechanism, thereby improving the overall performance of the architecture. This model surpasses the leading methods, achieving higher recognition rates and improved accuracy.

Deep learning-based models are composed of complex architectures that require more system resources, which leads to a higher computational cost. Zanobya and Jamil [26] proposed a lightweight CNN with multiple heads, each induced with a Squeeze and Excitation (SE) module to serve as an attention mechanism to automatically highlight salient features from limited training data while suppressing unimportant ones. The findings indicated that the suggested multiple-headed CNN architecture integrated with an attention module demonstrated improved performance compared to those without attention multi-head CNN and current state-of-the-art approaches. However, this model still needs improvement, as the proposed approach had trouble differentiating between various activities. Therefore, an optimal window size needs to be properly selected to address such a problem.

Yin *et al.* [27] proposed a parallel multi-headed CNN-BiLSTM that incorporated an attention mechanism even when encountering noisy data. Equal time sliding window size was adopted to address the problem encountered by the model proposed by Zanobya and Jamil [26]. The proposed model employed a parallel structure to reduce time complexity and a CNN-based bi-LSTM network to eliminate noisy data and reduce dimensionality. It also used an attention mechanism to achieve a better recognition rate by redistributing the weights of important representations. Its performance in contrast to other state-of-the-art architectures indicated that such proposed model performed relatively well on three publicly available datasets.

Many of the existing deep learning models are built upon some complex architectures and multiple hyperparameters. Numerous CNN architectures are employed as a baseline for HAR. Mekruksavanich and Jitpattanakul [28] proposed a hybridized CNN architecture that employed a channel attention mechanism to capture both spatial and sequential features for action recognition in daily living. It combined the capabilities of CNN-based ResNet architecture and bidirectional GRU attached with a squeeze and excitation module (SE). The hybrid model performed better on evaluation measures than other DL models, indicating that it is more accurate than the others.

Gao *et al*. [29] introduced DanHAR, a dual-attention model designed for Human Activity Recognition (HAR) that utilized multimodal wearable sensors. This model enhanced activity recognition by employing both channel and temporal attention mechanisms within a residual Convolutional Neural Network (CNN). The incorporation of a residual network served as the foundational architecture, allowing the model to focus on pertinent sensor modalities through channel attention, while temporal attention helped in emphasizing significant time steps in extensive sensor sequences. Although the introduction of dual attention added a layer of complexity, the model demonstrated substantial performance improvements across multiple datasets, with the computational overhead deemed negligible.

Buffelli and Vandin [30] proposed TrASenD, a novel framework for HAR that substitutes Rrecurrent Neural Networks (RNNs) with a purely attention-based mechanism. This shift enhances the model's capability to capture long-term dependencies in sensor data. Additionally, the framework includes a personalization component that tailors models to individual users *via* transfer learning. By employing an attention mechanism, TrASenD overcomes the limitations of RNNs in managing lengthy input sequences, particularly in multimodal sensor data scenarios. However, the model's ability to generalize may be challenged in contexts with high variability in sensor data among users, as effective transfer learning necessitates additional user-specific data, which may not always be accessible.

Laitrakun [31] proposed the Merging-Squeeze-Excitation (MSE) feature fusion technique, inspired by the Squeeze-and-Excitation (SE) block, for HAR with wearable sensors. The MSE method focuses on recalibrating feature maps to highlight essential features while diminishing the influence of irrelevant ones during the fusion of multimodal sensor data. This approach involves three main steps: pre-merging, squeeze-and-excitation, and post-merging. Evaluated using three deep learning architectures (LeNet5, AlexNet, VGG16) and four merging operations (addition, maximum, minimum, and average), the MSE method achieved the highest accuracy with AlexNet across multiple datasets, including PAMAP2, DaLiAc, and DSAD, effectively enhancing classification performance by emphasizing relevant features.

Akter *et al*. [32] introduced a new HAR classification method that incorporates attention mechanisms within a deep learning framework, particularly utilizing Convolutional Neural Networks (CNNs). This model integrates features from various convolutional stages and employs attention modules (CBAM) to improve feature extraction. A lightweight 2D CNN architecture was proposed that incorporates attention mechanisms to refine features throughout the training process. Instead of relying on manually crafted features, the model utilizes spectrograms derived from raw sensor data, demonstrating improved accuracy and computational efficiency when tested on three datasets (KU-HAR, UCI-HAR, and WISDM). The implementation of attention mechanisms (CBAM) significantly enhances the model's focus on critical features, leading to superior performance across various datasets.

CONCLUSION

This chapter explored and analyzed the recent advances in machine and deep learning algorithms that effectively categorize human actions from sensor-generated datasets. Deep learning-based models are proven to be more effective than models based on machine learning when classifying and categorizing human actions. Convolutional Neural Networks (CNNs) and Long Short-Term Memory (LSTM) are applied to carry out such tasks. However, the hybrid combination of such models is more effective than the baseline algorithm regarding accuracy and various other performance metrics. The attention mechanism, when incorporated with the CNN head, significantly boosts the performance of the model whenever applied. It has been observed that the squeeze and excitation module can be effectively utilized as an attention mechanism to focus on important feature maps within a CNN architecture by recalibrating those feature maps adaptively within the network. It does not only enhance the accuracy of a model but also the complexity of the attached model.

REFERENCES

[1]   A. Vaswani, N. Shazeer, N. Parmar, J. Uszkoreit, L. Jones, A. N. Gomez, Ł. Kaiser, and I. Polosukhin, "Attention is all you need," In: *Adv. Neural Inf. Process. Syst.*, vol. 30, 2017.

[2]   S.P. Singh, M.K. Sharma, A. Lay-Ekuakille, D. Gangwar, and S. Gupta, "Deep ConvLSTM with self-attention for human activity decoding using wearable sensors", *IEEE Sens. J.,* vol. 21, no. 6, pp. 8575-8582, 2021.
        [http://dx.doi.org/10.1109/JSEN.2020.3045135]

[3]   S. Gupta, "Deep learning based human activity recognition (HAR) using wearable sensor data", *Int. J. Inf. Manag. Data Insights,* vol. 1, no. 2, p. 100046, 2021.
        [http://dx.doi.org/10.1016/j.jjimei.2021.100046]

[4]   E. De-La-Hoz-Franco, P. Ariza-Colpas, J.M. Quero, and M. Espinilla, "Sensor-based datasets for human activity recognition–a systematic review of literature", *IEEE Access,* vol. 6, pp. 59192-59210, 2018.
        [http://dx.doi.org/10.1109/ACCESS.2018.2873502]

[5]   H.F. Nweke, Y.W. Teh, M.A. Al-garadi, and U.R. Alo, "Deep learning algorithms for human activity recognition using mobile and wearable sensor networks: State of the art and research challenges", *Expert Syst. Appl.,* vol. 105, pp. 233-261, 2018.
        [http://dx.doi.org/10.1016/j.eswa.2018.03.056]

[6]   T. M. Mitchell, and T. M. Mitchell, *Machine learning.,* vol. 9, McGraw-hill New York, 1997.

[7]   M. Ehatisham-Ul-Haq, A. Javed, M.A. Azam, H.M.A. Malik, A. Irtaza, I.H. Lee, and M.T. Mahmood, "Robust human activity recognition using multimodal feature-level fusion", *IEEE Access,* vol. 7, pp.

60736-60751, 2019.
[http://dx.doi.org/10.1109/ACCESS.2019.2913393]

[8]   N. Ahmed, J.I. Rafiq, and M.R. Islam, "Enhanced human activity recognition based on smartphone sensor data using hybrid feature selection model", *Sensors (Basel),* vol. 20, no. 1, p. 317, 2020.
[http://dx.doi.org/10.3390/s20010317] [PMID: 31935943]

[9]   P. Randhawa, V. Shanthagiri, A. Kumar, and V. Yadav, "Human activity detection using machine learning methods from wearable sensors", *Sens. Rev.,* vol. 40, no. 5, pp. 591-603, 2020.
[http://dx.doi.org/10.1108/SR-02-2020-0027]

[10]   A. Subasi, K. Khateeb, T. Brahimi, and A. Sarirete, "Human activity recognition using machine learning methods in a smart healthcare environment", *Innov. health inform.,* Elsevier, pp. 123-144, 2020.
[http://dx.doi.org/10.1016/B978-0-12-819043-2.00005-8]

[11]   A. Logacjov, K. Bach, A. Kongsvold, H.B. Bårdstu, and P.J. Mork, "HARTH: a human activity recognition dataset for machine learning", *Sensors (Basel),* vol. 21, no. 23, p. 7853, 2021.
[http://dx.doi.org/10.3390/s21237853] [PMID: 34883863]

[12]   D. Garcia-Gonzalez, D. Rivero, E. Fernandez-Blanco, and M.R. Luaces, "New machine learning approaches for real-life human activity recognition using smartphone sensor-based data", *Knowl. Base. Syst.,* vol. 262, p. 110260, 2023.
[http://dx.doi.org/10.1016/j.knosys.2023.110260]

[13]   A. Hayat, F. Morgado-Dias, B. Bhuyan, and R. Tomar, "Human activity recognition for elderly people using machine and deep learning approaches", *Information (Basel),* vol. 13, no. 6, p. 275, 2022.
[http://dx.doi.org/10.3390/info13060275]

[14]   A. Moin, A. Zhou, A. Rahimi, A. Menon, S. Benatti, G. Alexandrov, S. Tamakloe, J. Ting, N. Yamamoto, Y. Khan, F. Burghardt, L. Benini, A.C. Arias, and J.M. Rabaey, "A wearable biosensing system with in-sensor adaptive machine learning for hand gesture recognition", *Nat. Electron.,* vol. 4, no. 1, pp. 54-63, 2020.
[http://dx.doi.org/10.1038/s41928-020-00510-8]

[15]   S. Wan, L. Qi, X. Xu, C. Tong, and Z. Gu, "Deep learning models for real-time human activity recognition with smartphones", *Mob. Netw. Appl.,* vol. 25, no. 2, pp. 743-755, 2020.
[http://dx.doi.org/10.1007/s11036-019-01445-x]

[16]   Z. Qin, Y. Zhang, S. Meng, Z. Qin, and K.K.R. Choo, "Imaging and fusing time series for wearable sensor-based human activity recognition", *Inf. Fusion,* vol. 53, pp. 80-87, 2020.
[http://dx.doi.org/10.1016/j.inffus.2019.06.014]

[17]   S. Mekruksavanich, and A. Jitpattanakul, "Lstm networks using smartphone data for sensor-based human activity recognition in smart homes", *Sensors (Basel),* vol. 21, no. 5, p. 1636, 2021.
[http://dx.doi.org/10.3390/s21051636] [PMID: 33652697]

[18]   O. Nafea, W. Abdul, G. Muhammad, and M. Alsulaiman, "Sensor-based human activity recognition with spatio-temporal deep learning", *Sensors (Basel),* vol. 21, no. 6, p. 2141, 2021.
[http://dx.doi.org/10.3390/s21062141] [PMID: 33803891]

[19]   K. Xia, J. Huang, and H. Wang, "LSTM-CNN architecture for human activity recognition", *IEEE Access,* vol. 8, pp. 56855-56866, 2020.
[http://dx.doi.org/10.1109/ACCESS.2020.2982225]

[20]   I.U. Khan, S. Afzal, and J.W. Lee, "Human activity recognition *via* hybrid deep learning based model"., *Sensors (Basel),* vol. 22, no. 1, p. 323, 2022.
[http://dx.doi.org/10.3390/s22010323] [PMID: 35009865]

[21]   N. Dua, S.N. Singh, and V.B. Semwal, "Multi-input CNN-GRU based human activity recognition using wearable sensors", *Computing,* vol. 103, no. 7, pp. 1461-1478, 2021.
[http://dx.doi.org/10.1007/s00607-021-00928-8]

[22]   S.K. Challa, A. Kumar, and V.B. Semwal, "A multibranch CNN-BiLSTM model for human activity recognition using wearable sensor data", *Vis. Comput.*, vol. 38, no. 12, pp. 4095-4109, 2022.
[http://dx.doi.org/10.1007/s00371-021-02283-3]

[23]   D. Garcia-Gonzalez, D. Rivero, E. Fernandez-Blanco, and M.R. Luaces, "Deep learning models for real-life human activity recognition from smartphone sensor data", *Internet of Things*, vol. 24, p. 100925, 2023.
[http://dx.doi.org/10.1016/j.iot.2023.100925]

[24]   C. Dai, X. Liu, and J. Lai, "Human action recognition using two-stream attention based LSTM networks", *Appl. Soft Comput.*, vol. 86, p. 105820, 2020.
[http://dx.doi.org/10.1016/j.asoc.2019.105820]

[25]   K. Muhammad, Mustaqeem, A. Ullah, A.S. Imran, M. Sajjad, M.S. Kiran, G. Sannino, and V.H.C. de Albuquerque, "Human action recognition using attention based LSTM network with dilated CNN features", *Future Gener. Comput. Syst.*, vol. 125, pp. 820-830, 2021.
[http://dx.doi.org/10.1016/j.future.2021.06.045]

[26]   N.K. Zanobya, and A. Jamil, "Attention induced multi-head convolutional neural network for human activity recognition [J]", *Appl. Soft Comput.*, p. 110, 2021.

[27]   X. Yin, Z. Liu, D. Liu, and X. Ren, "A Novel CNN-based Bi-LSTM parallel model with attention mechanism for human activity recognition with noisy data", *Sci. Rep.*, vol. 12, no. 1, p. 7878, 2022.
[http://dx.doi.org/10.1038/s41598-022-11880-8] [PMID: 35550570]

[28]   S. Mekruksavanich, and A. Jitpattanakul, "Hybrid convolution neural network with channel attention mechanism for sensor-based human activity recognition", *Sci. Rep.*, vol. 13, no. 1, p. 12067, 2023.
[http://dx.doi.org/10.1038/s41598-023-39080-y] [PMID: 37495634]

[29]   W. Gao, L. Zhang, Q. Teng, J. He, and H. Wu, "DanHAR: Dual attention network for multimodal human activity recognition using wearable sensors", *Appl. Soft Comput.*, vol. 111, p. 107728, 2021.
[http://dx.doi.org/10.1016/j.asoc.2021.107728]

[30]   D. Buffelli, and F. Vandin, "Attention-based deep learning framework for human activity recognition with user adaptation", *IEEE Sens. J.*, vol. 21, no. 12, pp. 13474-13483, 2021.
[http://dx.doi.org/10.1109/JSEN.2021.3067690]

[31]   S. Laitrakun, "Merging-squeeze-excitation feature fusion for human activity recognition using wearable sensors", *Appl. Sci. (Basel)*, vol. 13, no. 4, p. 2475, 2023.
[http://dx.doi.org/10.3390/app13042475]

[32]   M. Akter, S. Ansary, M.A.M. Khan, and D. Kim, "Human activity recognition using attention-mechanism-based deep learning feature combination", *Sensors (Basel)*, vol. 23, no. 12, p. 5715, 2023.
[http://dx.doi.org/10.3390/s23125715] [PMID: 37420881]

CHAPTER 3

Classification of Acute Leukemia and Myeloid Neoplasm Using ResNet

Gowroju Swathi[1,*] and **G. Jyothi**[2]

[1] *Department of Computer Science and Engineering (AI and ML), Sreyas Institute of Engineering and Technology, Nagole, Hyderabad, India*

[2] *Department of Computer Science and Engineering (DS), Sreyas Institute of Engineering and Technology, Nagole, Hyderabad, India*

Abstract: An extensive comparison of cutting-edge image processing and machine learning methods for leukemia identification and classification is presented in this chapter. The proposed approach incorporates a thorough, extensive analytical approach that includes morphological operations, watershed segmentation, Wiener filtering, K-means clustering, and Gaussian filtration. By fine-tuning microscopic medical images, these preprocessing techniques enable accurate feature extraction and categorization. Using a multi-class Support Vector Machine (SVM) model, a total of 20 sub-features, including morphological, visual, and statistical characteristics, are retrieved and categorized. The proposed approach effectively classifies Acute Lymphoblastic Leukemia (ALL), Acute Myeloid Leukemia (AML), Chronic Lymphocytic Leukemia (CLL), Chronic Myeloid Leukemia (CML), and normal cells with a detection accuracy of 97.06% when tested on a dataset of 250 samples. To demonstrate the efficacy of the proposed approach, it is compared to state-of-the-art methods. The current method achieves 91.2% accuracy for ALL. By providing a scalable, effective, and precise method for leukemia identification and categorization, this study discusses advanced computer-aided diagnostic tools. The findings highlight how machine learning and image processing technology may enhance medical diagnostics by helping medical practitioners identify leukemia subtypes early and accurately.

Keywords: Classification, Deep learning, Leukemia, Lymphocytes, Neoplasm, Segmentation, White blood cells.

INTRODUCTION

White blood cells (WBC), known as "blasts," which are immature and irregularly shaped, are produced abnormally during the course of leukemia, a type of malignancy. White blood cells in a blood smear are often examined under a

---

[*] **Corresponding author Swathi Gowroju:** Department of CSE(AI&ML), Sreyas Institute of Engineering and Technology, Nagole, Hyderabad, India; E-mail: swathigowroju@sreyas.ac.in

Ashwani Kumar, Mohit Kumar, Avinash Kumar Sharma & Yojna Arora (Eds.)
All rights reserved-© 2025 Bentham Science Publishers

microscope to aid in diagnosis [1 - 6]. The proportion of RBC to WBC in an adult remains at 1000:1, and any figure above this mark indicates the presence ofleukemia in the patient. Hematologists use microscopic morphological and histological differences in blood smear cells to determine the kind and diagnosis of leukemia. Acute and chronic types of leukemia are the two major categories. The severe condition known as acute leukemia is characterized by a sharp rise in the proportion of abnormal cells in the patient's blood [7]. A biopsy test reveals high amounts of cells together with low concentrations of healthy white blood cells. Conversely, chronic leukemia typically progresses gradually [8]. Leukemic cells remain functional and carry out their natural tasks in the early stages, but as the disease progresses, the cells suffer substantial impairment. The patients experience symptoms such as weariness and nausea, and the primary diagnosis is made as a result of abnormal blood test findings. Inevitably, leukemia cells will outweigh healthy blood cells [9] and compromise systemic function if untreated. People with acute leukemia [10] have weariness, easy bruising, and frequent infections as symptoms.

Based on thorough scientific data, the World Health Organization (WHO) offers a categorization system for cancers. This system encompasses cancers that impact several organ systems and is a worldwide reference for clinical diagnosis, research, cancer registries, and public health monitoring. The most recent version, the fifth edition, advances the work that started more than 60 years ago by gathering all human tumors into a single relational database. This unique paradigm applies taxonomic principles along with key requirements, such as process transparency, bibliographic rigor, and bias avoidance, to classify tumors hierarchically across all organ systems and volumes (blue books).

An editorial board that oversees the creation of the 5th edition is made up of highly qualified individuals appointed for their leadership and current expertise pertinent to a particular volume, along with standing members who oversee the entire series and are participants from major medical and scientific organizations worldwide. The editorial board then chooses writers using a well-informed bibliometric method, placing a focus on trans-disciplinary knowledge and a wide geographic representation. To establish conceptual coherence and content harmonization, interdisciplinary writer/editor groups (a total of 420 participants) intentionally shared overlaps in the coverage of disease categories. Prior to 2001, numerous different and frequently disputed approaches were chosen to classify lymphomas, leukemia, and chronic myeloid diseases. Pathologists took the lead in classifying lymphoma using single skilled or neighborhood classifications, including those put forth by Rappaport, Lennert (Kiel), Lukes and Collins, and others. The Working Formulation, initially developed to standardize classification terminology, eventually evolved into its own classification system.

Hematologists have played a major role in the categorization of leukemias and myeloid diseases, with notable contributions from organizations like the Polycythemia Vera Study Group and the French-American-British (FAB) Cooperative Group. Leukemias and chronic myeloid diseases were also included in Rappaport's 1966 fascicle for the Military Institute of Pathology, which reflected early attempts to classify these ailments in a systematic manner. The criteria used to classify these tumors varied and were based on various combinations of clinical characteristics, cell morphology, cytochemical analyses and, in some cases, restricted immune phenotyping, frequently with little to no consideration of prognostic importance. Despite these drawbacks, the multiple classifications offered crucial diagnostic criteria for a range of hematologic neoplasms, enabling continued research and improvement. However, none of these categorizations represented a global consensus or included significant involvement from haematology experts.

Our goal is to develop a model to predict leukemia cells from cell images. We will approach this problem using two different methods:

Method 1: Build a basic Convolutional Neural Network (CNN) model using Keras.

Method 2: Use a pre-trained model to extract features from the images, then train traditional machine learning models on the extracted tabular features to solve the classification task.

LITERATURE SURVEY

Depending on the cell types involved, leukemia is further divided into subtypes. This additional classification indicates whether it is lymphoid or myeloid in origin. Lymphoid leukemia cells collect and result in lymph node enlargement, and immature white blood cells from the myeloid lineage proliferate out of control in Myeloid Leukemia (ML), especially Acute Myeloid Leukemia (AML). Leukemic cells can sometimes accumulate into solid masses known as myeloid sarcomas, also called chloromas. The four main types of leukemia are Acute Lymphocytic Leukemia (ALL), Persistent Lymphoid or Lymphoblastic Leukemia (PLL), Acute Myeloid Leukemia (AML), and Chronic Myeloid Leukemia (CML). The most frequent form of leukemia [14], known as ALL, accounts for about 12% of all instances of the disease, and its prevalence among children between the ages of 1 and 12 is 80%. Rapidly progressing ALL is distinguished by an abundance of embryonic leukocyte cells in the blood.

The examination of the ALL cells reveals that they contain a single nucleus and single nucleolus, as illustrated in Fig. (**1**). These cells are spherical and of uniform size. The severity of the leukemia is determined by using observed morphological patterns, raising the likelihood of automation by using Deep Learning (DL) and image processing techniques. Currently, in addition to total and differential white blood cell counts, microscopic examination of blood samples is a common practice in many developing countries to confirm and subtype leukemia. The most practical method for the initial screening of ALL is still the morphological analysis of stained blood films. Factors such as operator experience and fatigue can introduce bias in the microscopic technique, which relies on human inspection, leading to error rates as high as 40%. Therefore, a reliable automated solution for leukemia diagnosis is needed to minimize manual errors and reduce variability. We need a reliable solution to automatically diagnose leukemia in order to reduce manual error and variations. The parameters, such as sensitivity and specificity of the disease, are multiplied by the decision-making capabilities of Machine Learning (ML) approaches.

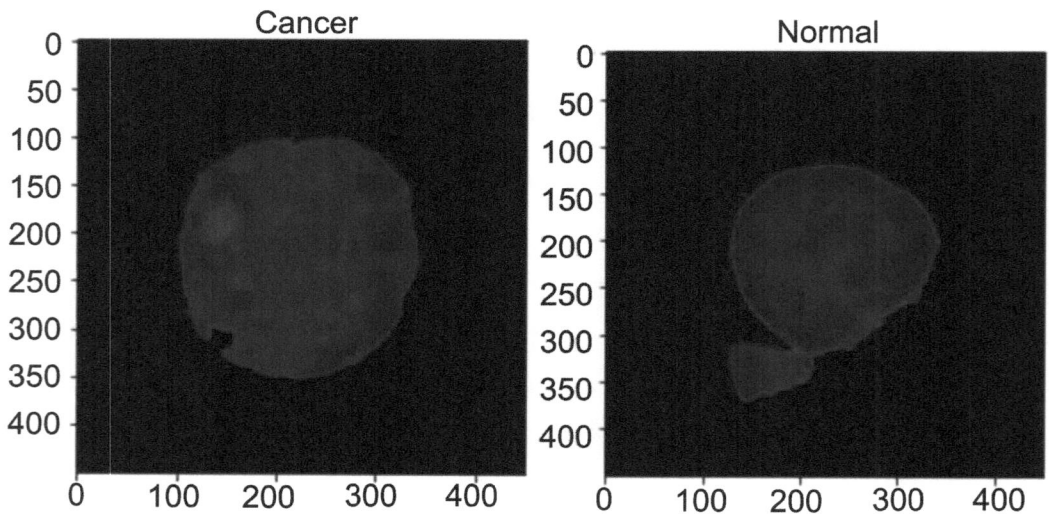

Fig. (1). Leukemia cancer and normal cell structures.

The promise of computational methods in differentiating leukemia types has been successfully demonstrated so far using a variety of image processing approaches, but the majority of these approaches focused primarily on ALL typing. Most recently, a study [15] employed fuzzy C-means clustering to diagnose Type 1 disease using a series of 19 images sourced from an online database, achieving 90% accuracy in about 2 minutes of processing time. The proposed system built an artificial neural network on a set of images that had already been preprocessed (*i.e.*, histogram equalized and canny edge detected) and obtained an accuracy of 97.8% in identifying lymphoblastic tumors.

PROPOSED IMPLEMENTATION

Proper preprocessing techniques are essential for preparing the collected microscopic images, often requiring the removal of irrelevant or noisy regions. This section provides a detailed explanation of the preprocessing methods used for white blood cell (WBC) segmentation, followed by the feature extraction and classification approaches applied in this study. Fig. (**2**) illustrates the overall workflow and block diagram used to develop the system.

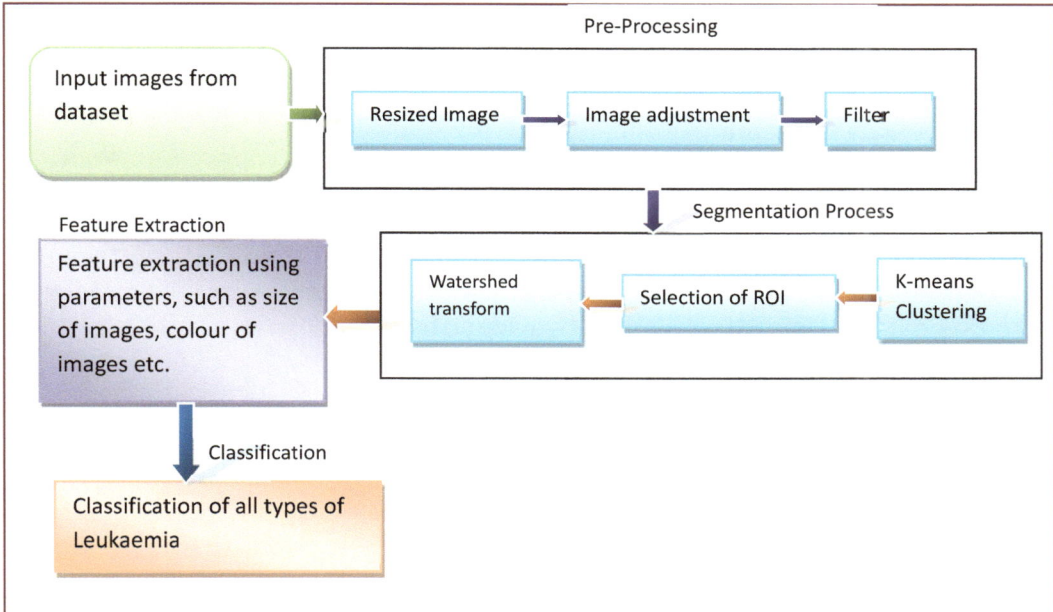

Fig. (2). Proposed architecture.

Dataset

ALL is the most prevalent kind of cancer in children, accounting for almost 25% of all pediatric malignancies [16]. The diagnosis is made by segmenting aberrant lymphoblasts in microscopic images of bone marrow samples or blood smears. However, there are a number of difficulties with this process. It can be challenging to precisely identify and segment the cells due to staining noise caused by inconsistent dye delivery, which can result in uneven coloring and visual distortions. Similar to this, poor lighting during imaging can cause illumination artifacts, which can obscure cellular features by producing overexposed or underexposed areas. The accuracy of automated image processing methods used for cell segmentation may be hampered by these issues. Notwithstanding these drawbacks, significant adjustments are frequently made to improve image quality at the acquisition stage, guaranteeing improved leukemia detection and classification. They are a good representation of images in the real world. There are numerous cell images in the dataset. The following procedures describe the organization and preparation of a dataset for training and evaluating a model, particularly for image data.

1. Three folders were created for the main data: Train, Test, and Validation.
2. Folders fold_0, fold_1, and fold_2 were all included in the training folder.
3. Each fold had two distinct folders: all and hem.
4. Discussion of the dataset led us to the conclusion that the hem files contain photos devoid of leukemia cells.
5. Researchers must do these divisions.
6. Image formats were .bmp
7. All photos used a 3-channel (8-bit) RGB encoding.

Due to their physical resemblance, young leukemic blasts and normal cells can be difficult to distinguish under a microscope, which is why an experienced oncologist annotated the labels. A total of 15,135 images were obtained altogether from 118 patients and divided into two identified classes: leukemia blast and normal cell.

Image Preprocessing

Fig. (**3**) shows the cell distribution from a bone marrow smear or stained blood sample used to diagnose ALL. It is difficult to distinguish leukemic blasts from normal cells using microscopy because of their comparable physical characteristics, particularly in the absence of sophisticated image processing methods. To deal with variances caused by staining artifacts and inconsistent illumination in microscope images, preprocessing techniques, including noise reduction, color normalization, and contrast modification, are frequently utilized. There were 15130 images altogether from 118 patients, divided into two identified classes: leukemia blast (Fig. **2**) and normal cells.

By removing dark regions from the images, we reduce the number of pixels the model must process during training and testing. This can be interpreted as eliminating irrelevant features from the dataset. This preprocessing step offers several advantages, including:

• Less memory is required to load photos.
• Fewer features are required to train a model.
• Less memory is required to train the model (fewer model weights are used).
• Due to fewer unnecessary characteristics, our model will learn more quickly.

• Fewer features mean that our model will learn more quickly (more features equal more processing calculations).

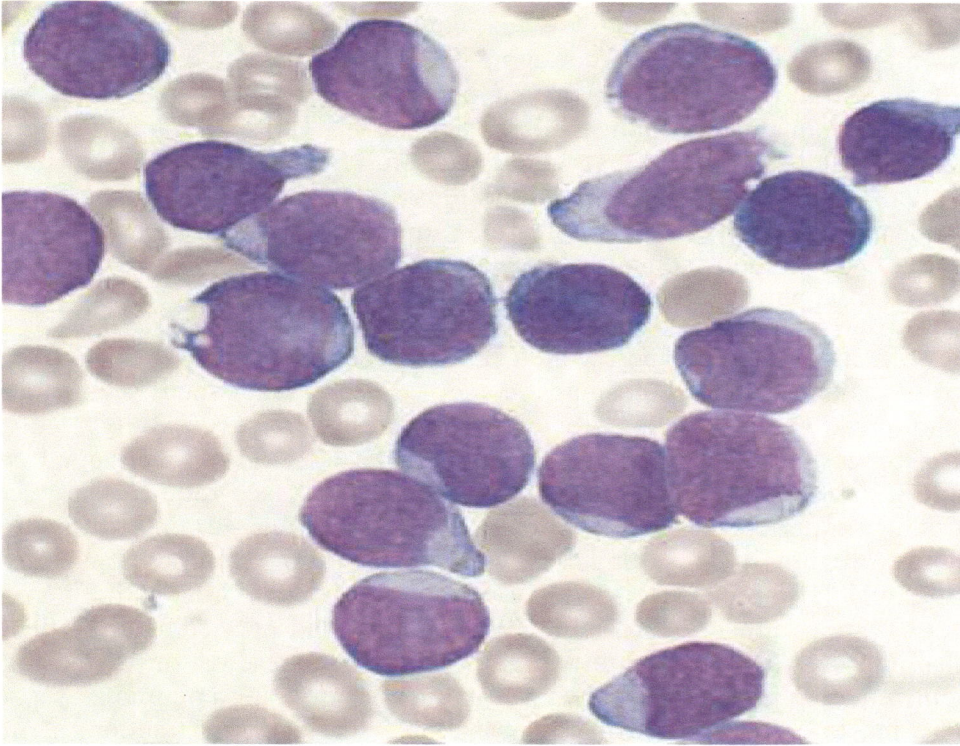

Fig. (3). Cell distribution in the blood.

The excessive inconsistencies resulting from the staining process frequently resulted in noise in the produced images. Prior to segmentation, pre-processing was used to clean up undesirable segments and background noise from the blood image in order to improve image quality. The original RGB image, which was 2592 by 1944 pixels in size, was shrunk to 500 by 500 pixels as part of the pre-processing step using the methods. Image improvement step two involved scaling and normalizing the image intensity to a range of 0 to 1. After that, to lessen the effect of camera noise and incorrect pixel values in the microscopic pictures, a Gaussian filter was used. By using a Gaussian function to smooth the picture, the Gaussian filter lowered high-frequency noise while maintaining crucial elements like cell borders. This produced consistent lighting. As a result, the image received a homogenous illumination field. To reduce noise and blur, the "Median" and "Wiener" filters were sequentially used. Particularly, the Wiener filter [22] reduced the MSE in the images.

Image Segmentation

The most important stage in the picture analysis is segmenting the WBCs and RBCs like background particles because leukemia is characterized by aberrant WBs. In the later stages, effective segmentation yields accurate findings. The K-means algorithm was employed in our proposed system to separate the white blood cells from the red blood cells and platelets. The overlapping generated white blood cells (lymphocytes) were successfully separated using the marker-controlled watershed segmentation algorithms with erosion and dilation features. K-means was chosen because it performs more quickly than basic segmentation using the Otsu method. Some of the leukocytes and other cells are visible in the digital microscope's photos.

Cells with incomplete shapes, which hinder accurate feature extraction, were removed using a border-cleaning method. Before watershed segmentation, morphological operations like erosion and dilation were successfully used. The erosion process reduced the overlapping boundary region of overlapped cells, leaving just a small number of pixels to indicate the fused region. The nuclear regions also experienced size reduction due to erosion (Fig. **4a**), in addition to the membrane regions. The boundaries were restored to their previous size by dilation, which is applied worldwide to add more pixels in order to fight erosion (Fig. **4b**). In contrast to erosion, area opening was applied to significantly overlapping cells (Fig. **4c**), providing an accurate representation of the region without reducing its size. To prevent 'vacuoles' from being counted as separate entities and to create a uniform region suitable for feature extraction, a filling operation was performed on the image. These preprocessing steps were used to convert RGB images into binary format, as illustrated in Fig. (**4**).

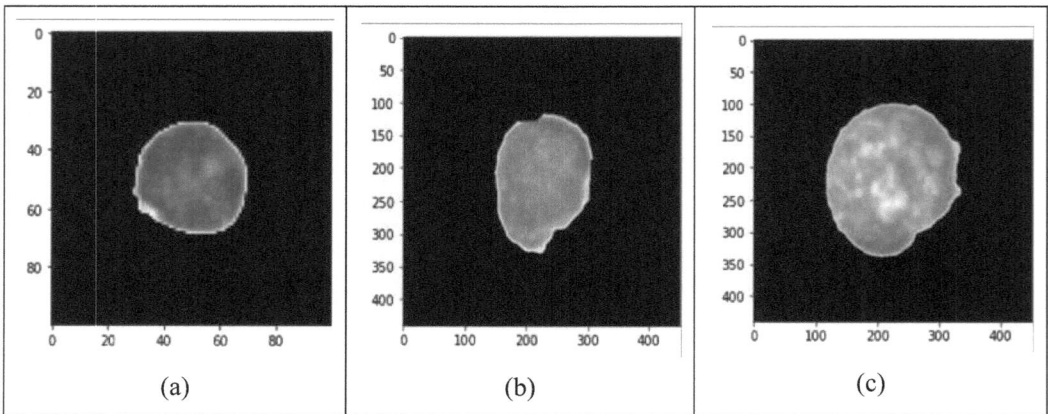

(a)   (b)   (c)

Fig. (4). Morphologically processed images.

Feature Extraction

After a successful preprocessing step, features were extracted from the divided cytoplasm and nucleus. The size, quantity, color, shape, and chromatic organization of the leukemia cells were among the primary qualities that the feature extraction concentrated on since hematologists distinguish blasts from healthy white blood cells based on these characteristics. The accuracy of the descriptors used to accurately reflect the mathematical, textural, and color aspects of the cells is crucial for a computer-aided diagnostic system's success. In this step, the categorization of the type of leukemia depends on the removal of duplicate characteristics and unnecessary data. Only the descriptors that distinguish the classes more effectively are kept.

Classification

Classification is the process of inquiring or associating a new test vector with a recognised class. It is possible to classify the provided sample set of malignant and healthy cells using ML methods. A Support Vector Machine (SVM) was used for this work because of its efficacy, outperforming earlier techniques, such as Artificial Neural Networks (ANN) and K-Nearest Neighbors (KNN). Moreover, it is especially helpful for binary classification tasks, such as differentiating between cancerous and healthy cells. Support vectors, which are derived from training examples and are known as hyperplanes, were also utilized in addition to class descriptors. Similar to cutting the positive sample from the negative samples, these hyperplanes, which are mathematically defined as Eq. (**1**), split the true samples from the negative samples in a manner comparable to a line dividing a two-dimensional plane into two parts.

$$f(x) = \beta0 + \beta(x) \tag{1}$$

Where βx is bias or noise, and $\beta 0$ is the weight vector (x). The bias was found to be 0.3344 during the experimental implementation. The kernel, a set of functions used in this classifier, maps the input data into a higher-dimensional space, making it linearly separable. The radial basis function (RBF), also known as the support vector machine radial (SVM-R), was employed in this study. This method featured one free parameter that needed to be adjusted for the best classification results.

RESULTS

K-Means clustering is applied to separate the specific picture regions of interest, such as WBCs. The overlapping cells were correctly detected and labeled before the geometric characteristics of each cell were calculated. Boundary lines were traced on an image after segmentation to differentiate the cells in order to delineate overlaps. This was done using the marker-controlled watershed method. The technique uses nuclei-based segmentation to identify overlapping cells uniquely. After overlapping cells' nuclei were processed, each cell was separated and processed independently. In this investigation, the model was tested using about 25% of the 520 total images. Among them, a total of 10 photos and 30 x 4 = 120 photographs fell into the category of leukemia, respectively. For the categorization of cell types, respectively, an accuracy of 97.6%, 97.3%, 94.6%, 97.4%, and 98.6% was attained for ALL, AML, CLL, CML, and normal cell types in the testing phase using the SVM method.

As shown in Fig. (**5**), the dataset was not balanced. Some of the illustrations from both groups are shown in Fig. (**6**). The image shows six blood cells on a black backdrop. Every cell has a unique morphology; some seem more spherical, while others have irregular shapes. Given their crimson color, the cells could be dyed to make them easier to see. It is frequently linked to blood smear analysis, which may be used to diagnose blood diseases like leukemia. The distinct segmentation of the cells draws attention to their characteristics, utilized for additional categorization or computational research.

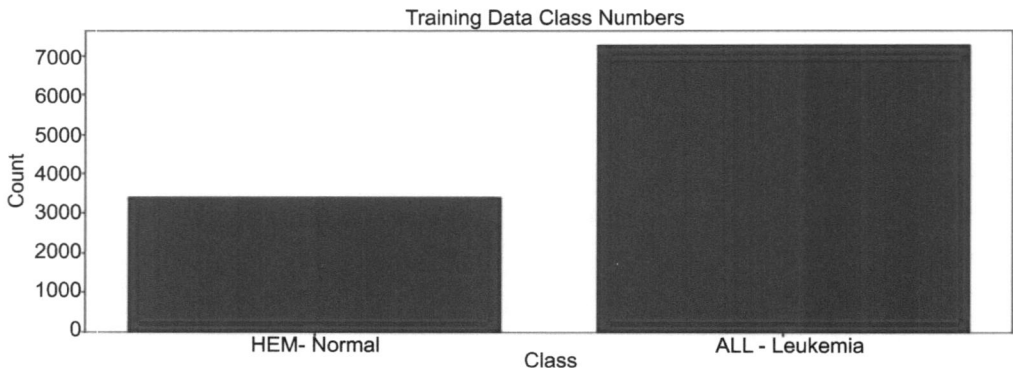

Fig. (5). Labeled classification count.

Getting Rid of Black Areas in Data

Removing dark regions reduces the number of pixels processed during model training and testing. This might be interpreted as removing pointless features from the dataset. This pre-process has many benefits, such as:

1. Less memory is required to load photos.
2. Fewer features are required to train a model.
3. Less memory is required to train the model (fewer model weights are used).

4. Due to fewer unnecessary characteristics, our model will learn more quickly.
5. Fewer features mean that our model will learn more quickly (more features equal more processing calculations).

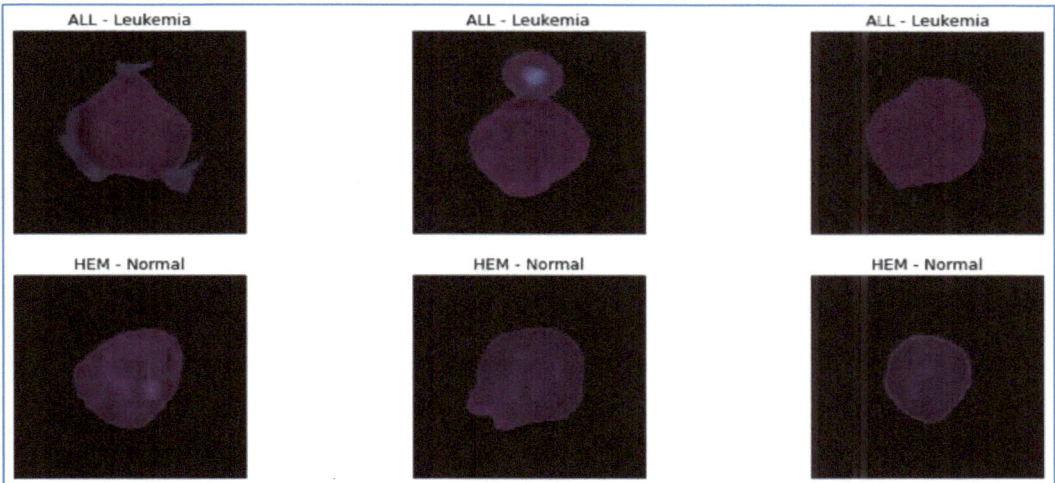

Fig. (6). Input images from the dataset.

Resize parameters can be considered hyperparameters, as they influence the final feature count per sample. To preserve the original height-to-width ratio, black padding is applied when resizing; otherwise, direct resizing may distort cell shapes, as shown in Fig. (**7**).

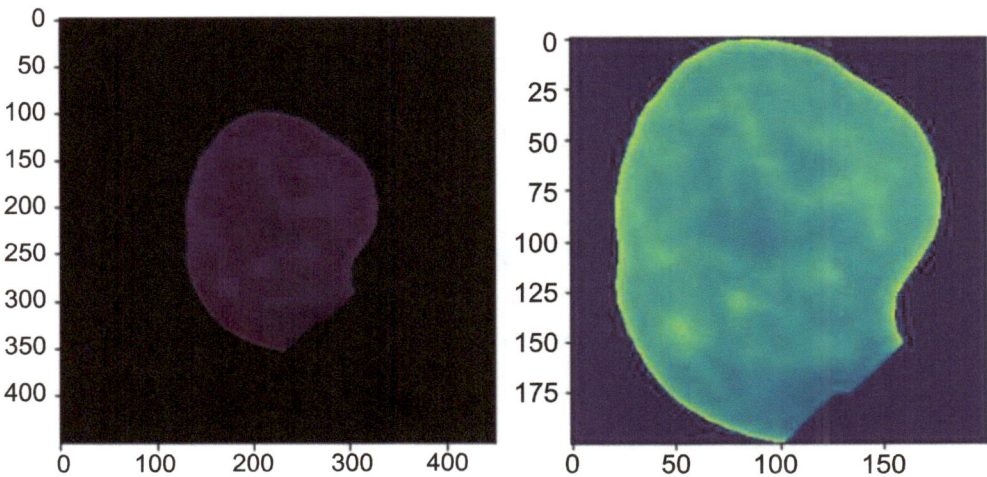

Fig. (7). Before crop and after crop from the left side.

In order to obtain some test data, we divided the data into a train set and a test set. Standard 8-bit colour means that each pixel has a value between 0 and 255. Therefore, we normalized our features (pixels) from 0 to 1 using the min-max normalized. We then employed an L2 dropout regularizer and simple CNN. In our model, batch normalization was also used. Initial tests indicate that the model is clearly overfitting, as evidenced by high training accuracy with low generalization. To address this, regularization techniques are necessary. Since the task is a binary classification problem, the output layer has a single neuron with a sigmoid activation function.

A portion of the outcome from the proposed system is shown in Fig. (**8**). The contrast-enhanced image, which was prepared using a Gaussian and Wiener filter in the preprocessing and feature extraction, is displayed next to the original input image. Fig. (**8**) illustrates how the contrast of the image is uneven and appears blurry. As a result, we eliminated the "salt and pepper" noise from the acquired image in order to normalize the contrast. KNN was used to segment the specific regions of interest in the image, such as WBCs. The intersecting cells were correctly detected and labeled before the geometric characteristics of each cell were calculated. Boundary lines were drawn on the resultant image to split cells in order to delineate overlaps. This was done using the marker-controlled watershed method. The technique used nuclei-based segmentation to identify overlapping cells uniquely. Cells were resolved and processed separately from the nuclei of any overlapping cells that have been recognized.

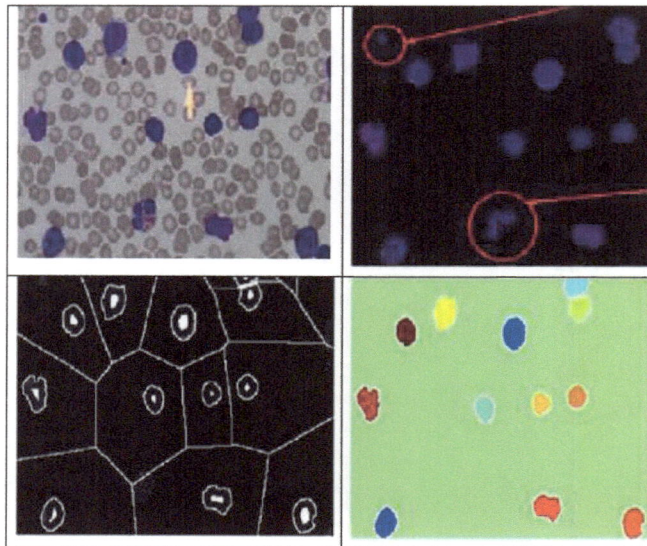

Fig. (8). Segmentation of cells.

To better understand the input data used for the pre-trained model, we display the data shape after obtaining it and just before extracting tabular features. According to the pre-trained model, the amount of features may change. In contrast to VGG19, ResNet50 obtained 2048 features. The training was performed using the convolutional neural network (CNN) model. Table **1** includes information on each layer's output shape, number of parameters, and related layers. In order to extract features, the model started with a sequence of 2D convolution layers with progressively larger filter sizes (2, 4, and 8 channels). MaxPooling layers then lowered the spatial dimensions, while dropout layers were used for regularization. Feature extraction was further improved with deeper layers, such as Conv2D with 16 and 24 filters. The data was flattened for input into dense layers after the convolutional blocks.

Table 1. Model summary while training the dataset.

Layer	Output Shape	No. of Parameters
Convolution 2D	200x20X0, 2	20
Convolution 2D_1	200x20X0, 4	86
Convolution 2D_2	200x20X0, 8	910
MaxPooling2D	100x10x0.8	0
Dropout	100x10x0.8	0
Conv2D	100x10x0.16	3216
MaxPooling2	50x50x16,0	0
Conv2D	50x50x24,0	18840
Dropout	50x50x24,0	0
Flatten	-	60000
Dense	-	4540064
batch_normalization	64	512
dense_1	32	3080
dense_2	32	1056
dense_3	1	33

The main trainable block is a fully connected (Dense) layer with 4540064 parameters. Dropout and batch normalization layers were used to stabilize training and avoid overfitting. This model architecture was designed for deep learning applications, such as image classification or medical imaging analysis, where effective feature extraction from 2D data is essential. The training performance (accuracy or potential loss), depicted in Fig. (**9a**), is shown by the blue line, which exhibits a generally steady trend with few oscillations. The validation performance with the orange line shows an irregular pattern, with a notable decline (which might be an indicator of a rapid reduction in accuracy or a quick increase in validation loss), followed by a rebound. This indicates that if a model performs well on training data but has trouble generalizing to validation data, it may be unstable or exhibiting signs of overfitting. Both the training (blue) and validation (orange) curves in Fig. (**9b**) show variations, although the validation curve's unpredictability is more noticeable. The validation metric exhibits abrupt peaks and valleys, which might be caused by batch volatility, model instability, or problems like noisy data or overfitting. The overall pattern indicates that while the training curve steadies with time, the validation performance is still erratic, which may indicate overfitting or the need for more effective regularization techniques.

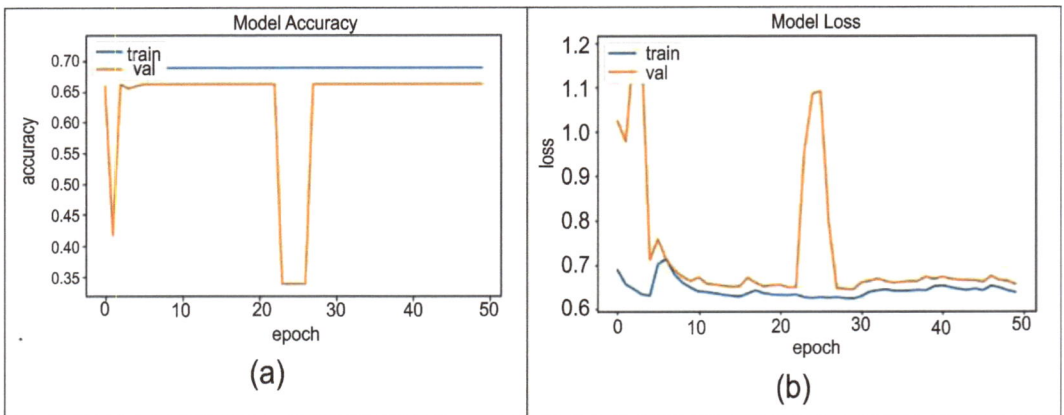

Fig. (9). Model accuracy and loss graphs.

The model effectively learns when the training loss (red) and validation loss (green) gradually decline with each epoch, as shown in Fig. (**10**). The model appears to be stabilizing with minimal overfitting as the loss curves converge towards the end. The best validation performance is indicated by a blue dot at epoch 15, which suggests that this may be the ideal epoch for minimizing loss. The model has successfully learned the training data, as evidenced by the training accuracy (red), which steadily rises to almost 1.0 (100%) by the end epoch. At epoch 14, which is designated as the best epoch with a blue dot, the validation accuracy (green) likewise exhibits an upward trend, peaking at about 95%. As shown in Table **2**, with a precision of 0.97, *i.e.*, 97% of the projected positives were accurate, and with a recall of 0.97, *i.e.*, 97% of the actual positive cases were correctly identified, the class 'All' performed well. As shown in Table **2**, the model maintained a decent trade-off between false positives and false negatives, as seen by the reported F1-score of 0.96, striking a compromise between accuracy and recall. The measurements were based on a significant number of real-world examples, with 1456 as evidence. With an overall accuracy of 97%, 97% of the 1500 occurrences were properly identified by the model. Furthermore, the weighted average (W_Avg) (which takes class imbalance into account) provided precision (P) scores of 0.95, recall (R) scores of 0.96, and F1-score (F1) of 0.94, but the micro-average (M-Avg) across classes demonstrated precision, recall, and F1-score of 0.96, 0.97, and 0.94, respectively.

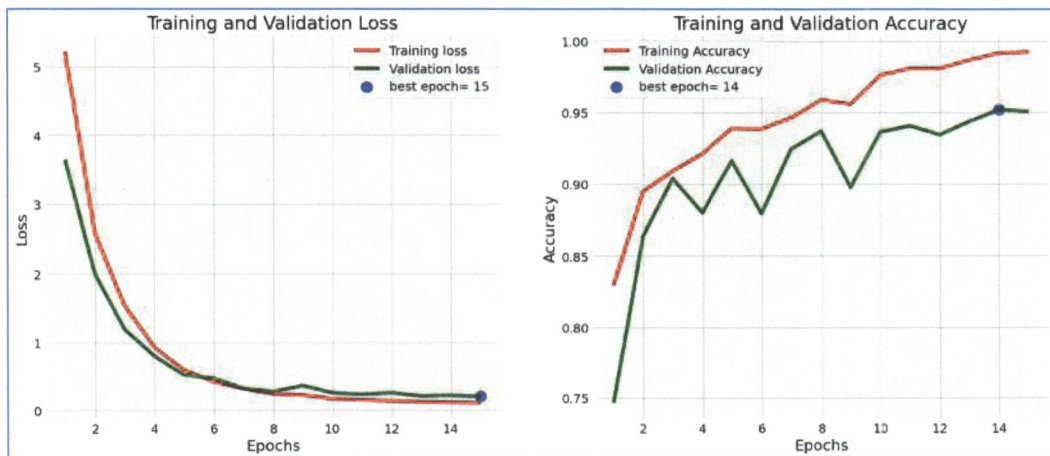

Fig. (10). Performance of the model.

Table 2. Evaluation parameters of the model.

-	P	R	F1
All	0.97	0.97	0.96
Accuracy	-	-	0.97
M-Avg	0.96	0.97	0.94
W_Avg	0.95	0.96	0.95

The categorization results are graphically represented by the confusion matrix in Fig. (**11**). It aids in evaluating how well the classifiers performed in identifying leukemia types from blood smear images. The True Positive (TP), True Negative (TN), False Positive (FP), and False Negative (FN) categories are produced by the matrix and are essential for computing performance measures.

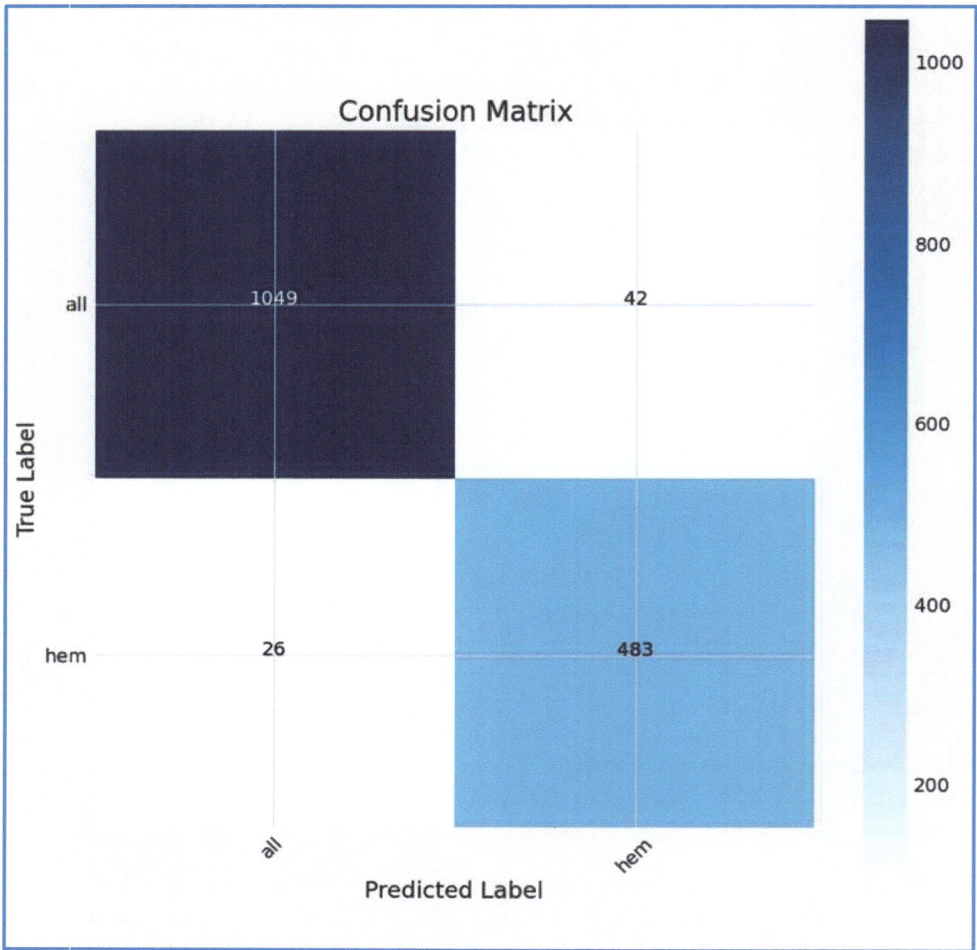

Fig. (11). Confusion matrix representation.

The performance metrics, as shown in Eq (**2**), Eq (**3**), and Eq (**4**), shed light on how well the classifiers differentiate between blasts and healthy white blood cells.

$$Accuracy = \frac{TP + TN}{TP + TN + FP + FN} \, X \, 100 \qquad (2)$$

$$Sensitivity = \frac{TP}{TP + FN} X100 \qquad (3)$$

$$Specificity = \frac{TN}{TN + FP} X100 \qquad (4)$$

Each of the five main data sets, namely normal, ALL, AML, CLL, and CML, underwent a separate learning or training process. To assess accuracy, specificity, and sensitivity, testing and validation were also carried out individually on those five data sets. The aggregate estimate for each measure was then produced by averaging all the readings.

DISCUSSION

We automatically identified ALL using the DCNN and divided its subtype into 4 groups. Since our proposed method does not need segmenting microscopic images compared to other feature extraction techniques, it performed well and outperformed earlier conventional methods. Convolution, hidden layers of DCNN, contribute to automatically recognizing and categorizing particular leukemia cells from a vast amount of microscopic image data.

Numerous state-of-the-art research works have proposed various leukemia detection methods; however, due to the high levels of intraclass heterogeneity and interclass similarity among leukemia subtypes, few of these studies have addressed subtype classification. Even though these subtypes are challenging to categories, they are vital for accurate disease diagnosis of leukemia.

In this pilot investigation, we carried out automatic ALL detection and divided its subtypes into 4 classifications. K-mean clustering was utilized to segment the images, and the SVM classifier was used to categories ALL subtypes once different features were extracted. They were able to detect leukemia with 97% accuracy on their particular data set and classify ALL subtypes with 95.6% accuracy.

Although it had little impact on the functionality of our proposed system, one of the limitations of our proposed system is that we neglected to suppress image noise. However, there are a variety of techniques available to minimize image noise, which could improve the algorithm's performance. These techniques include frequency filtering, Gaussian smoothing, conservative smoothing, median, mean, and unsharp filters. Additionally, we employed a small number of training and assessment data sets in this study, which can have an impact on how a deep neural network is trained. Table **3** presents the comparison of several research works on classifiers used for medical image detection and classification, including stain normalization methods, deep belief networks (DBN), support vector machines (SVM), and k-nearest neighbor (KNN) algorithms. With KNN plus the Hough Transform algorithm, Subhan *et al.* achieved the greatest subtype classification accuracy of 96.78%. The detection accuracy for these approaches ranged from 91.85% to 99.55%. A possible subject for more study and improvement is indicated by the fact that many studies do not address subtype categorization, even if the majority concentrate on overall detection accuracy. This chapter highlights how well a variety of classifiers work in medical image analysis, with KNN showing the best results in both detection and subtype classification.

Table 3. Comparison of classification accuracy with modern classifiers.

Study/Authors	Classifier Employed	ALL Detection Accuracy (%)	Subtype Classification Accuracy (%)
Gupta *et al.* [1]	Stain normalization techniques for microscopic medical images	91.85	Subtype classification not addressed
Duggal *et al.* [2]	Deep Belief Networks (DBN)	92.85	Subtype classification not addressed
Putzu *et al.* [3].	Image Processing Techniques and Support Vector Machine (SVM)	93.45	Subtype classification not addressed
Subhan *et al.* [4]	K-Nearest Neighbor (KNN) and the Hough Transform algorithm	96.54	96.78
Faivdullah *et al* [6].	Image Processing Algorithm	99.55	Subtype classification not addressed
Proposed Model	Deep Convolutional Neural Network (DCNN)	99.74	96.06

A comparative review of the numerous approaches used for leukemia detection and classification utilizing various algorithms and methodologies is presented in Table **4**. The maximum accuracy of 97.06% was attained by the proposed approach, incorporating preprocessing techniques, such as Gaussian filtering, K-means clustering, and several morphological processes. This proposed approach used 20 sub-features identified by a support vector machine (SVM) model to categorize subtypes, including ALL, AML, CLL, CML, and normal cells. Other techniques, such as those proposed by Dawwa *et al.*, employed the Zack algorithm that concentrates on texture, color, and geometry and detected ALL pictures with an accuracy of 91.2%. By using a KNN classifier with the Hough transform, Subhan *et al.* [4] were able to diagnose acute leukemia with 96.5% accuracy. Using a mix of statistical, color, and morphological data, Dawwa *et al.*, in another study, employed Zack's K-means method to detect both ALL and healthy cells with 94.3% accuracy. This comparative study demonstrated that the proposed method outperforms others by incorporating advanced preprocessing and classification algorithms to improve subtype categorization and detection accuracy.

Table 4. Comparison of the proposed system with existing state-of-art methods.

Author	Implementation Details	Feature Extraction and Classification	Test Sample Count	Result	Accuracy
Proposed Method	Preprocessing images using Gaussian filtration, K-means clustering with a Wiener filter, marker-based watershed segmentation, and morphological operations.	Morphological, visual, and statistical features were extracted. A total of 29 sub-features were detected by using SVMs.	250	Able to identify and categorise ALL, AML, CLL, CML, and normal cells.	97.06
Putzua *et al* [3].	Extend or equalize the contrast in the histogram.	Zack algorithm	Colour, geometry, and texture.	Able to detect ALL images.	91.2
Subhan *et al* [4].	Texture, statistical geometric, colour [totaling 18 sub-features].	KNN classifier under the Hough transform.	-	Able to detect acute leukemia.	96.5
Dumyan *et al.* [7]	Zack's k-means algorithm.	-	Statistical, colour, morphological features, texture, and 20 other sub-features.	Detect ALL and healthy cells.	94.3
Rawat *et al.* [5].	Threshold segmentation (Post-processing).	For morphological degradation, median filtering was applied.	NA	ALL and normal categories	96.2

CONCLUSION

A pre-trained deep convolutional neural network (DCNN) architecture was used in this study to identify and categorize acute lymphoblastic leukemia (ALL) and its subtypes. We obtained a 99.50% detection accuracy and a 96.06% subtype classification accuracy by using data augmentation. Early diagnosis enabled by this automated method can significantly improve treatment outcomes. In order to identify the best model for ALL diagnoses, future studies might concentrate on implementing and contrasting different deep learning architectures. Training deep learning models from scratch with bigger datasets is another exciting avenue that shows promise for improving the precision and resilience of these systems for practical uses. These technologies can help oncologists and pathologists by increasing the accuracy of diagnoses. A completely automated diagnostic system might be developed by incorporating the model as a sub-module with precisely specified input and output parameters, among other developments. Future studies may also focus on developing an automated system for acute myeloid leukemia (AML), with the goal of fully detecting all forms of blood malignancy.

REFERENCES

[1]   A. Gupta, R. Duggal, S. Gehlot, R. Gupta, A. Mangal, L. Kumar, N. Thakkar, and D. Satpathy, "GCTI-SN: Geometry-inspired chemical and tissue invariant stain normalization of microscopic medical images", *Med. Image Anal.,* vol. 65, p. 101788, 2020. [http://dx.doi.org/10.1016/j.media.2020.101788]

[2]   R. Duggal, A. Gupta, R. Gupta, M. Wadhwa, and C. Ahuja, "Overlapping cell nuclei segmentation in microscopic images using deep belief networks," In: *Proc. 10th Indian Conf. on Computer Vision, Graphics and Image Processing (ICVGIP)*, 2016, pp. 1–8. [http://dx.doi.org/10.1145/3009977.3010043]

[3]   L. Putzu, G. Caocci, and C. Di Ruberto, "Leucocyte classification for leukaemia detection using image processing techniques", *Artif. Intell. Med.,* vol. 62, no. 3, pp. 179-191, 2014. [http://dx.doi.org/10.1016/j.artmed.2014.09.002] [PMID: 25241903]

[4]   M.S. Subhan, and M.P. Kaur, "Significant analysis of leukemic cells extraction and detection using KNN and Hough transform algorithm", *International Journal of Computer Science Trends and Technology,* vol. 3, no. 1, pp. 27-33, 2015. [IJCST].

[5]   J. Rawat, A. Singh, H.S. Bhadauria, and J. Virmani, "H. S. Bhadauria, and Jitendra Virmani. "Computer aided diagnostic system for detection of leukemia using microscopic images."", *Procedia Comput. Sci.,* vol. 70, pp. 748-756, 2015. [http://dx.doi.org/10.1016/j.procs.2015.10.113]

[6]   L. Faivdullah, F. Azahar, Z.Z. Htike, and W.Y.N. Naing, "Leukemia detection from blood smears", *J. Med. Bioeng.,* vol. 4, no. 6, pp. 488-491, 2015. [http://dx.doi.org/10.12720/jomb.4.6.488-491]

[7]   S. Dumyan, and A. Gupta, "An enhanced technique for lymphoblastic cancer detection using artificial neural network", *International Journal of Advanced Research in Computer Science and Electronics Engineering,* vol. 6, no. 4, p. 38, 2017. [IJARCSEE].

[8]   S. Gowroju, S. Kumar, Aarti, and A. Ghimire, "Deep neural network for accurate age group prediction through pupil using the optimized unet model", *Math. Probl. Eng.,* vol. 2022, pp. 1-24, 2022. [http://dx.doi.org/10.1155/2022/7813701]

[9]   A. Swathi, Aarti, and S. Kumar, "A smart application to detect pupil for small dataset with low illumination", *Innov. Syst. Softw. Eng.,* vol. 17, no. 1, pp. 29-43, 2021. [http://dx.doi.org/10.1007/s11334-020-00382-3]

[10]   S. Gowroju, Aarti, and S. Kumar, "Review on secure traditional and machine learning algorithms for age prediction using IRIS image", *Multimedia Tools Appl.,* vol. 81, no. 24, pp. 35503-35531, 2022. [http://dx.doi.org/10.1007/s11042-022-13355-4]

[11]   S. Gowroju, "A novel implementation of fast phrase search for encrypted cloud storage", *IJSREM,* vol. 3, no. 09, 2019.

[12]   A. Swathi, "Intelligent fatigue detection by using ACS and by avoiding false alarms of fatigue detection", *In Innovations in Computer Science and Engineering: Proceedings of the Sixth ICICSE 2018,* 2019pp. 225-233

[13]   S. Gowroju, and S. Kumar, "Robust deep learning technique: U-Net architecture for pupil segmentation", *In 2020 11th IEEE annual information technology, electronics and mobile communication conference (IEMCON),* IEEE, pp. 0609-0613, 2020. [http://dx.doi.org/10.1109/IEMCON51383.2020.9284947]

[14] A. Swathi, V. Aarti, Y. Swathi, Sirisha, M. Rishitha, S. Tejaswi, L. Shashank Reddy, and M. Sujith Reddy, "A reliable novel approach of bio-image processing—age and gender prediction", *In proceedings of fourth international conference on computer and communication technologies: IC3T 2022,* Springer Nature Singapore: Singapore, pp. 329-336, 2023.

[15] A. Swathi, "Intelligent fatigue detection by using ACS and by avoiding false alarms of fatigue detection", *In Innovations in Computer Science and Engineering: Proceedings of the Sixth ICICSE 2018,* Springer Singapore, pp. 225-233, 2019.

[16] M. Aria, M. Ghaderzadeh, D. Bashash, H. Abolghasemi, F. Asadi, and A. Hosseini, Acute Lymphoblastic Leukemia (ALL) image dataset [Data set] [http://dx.doi.org/10.34740/KAGGLE/DSV/2175623]

[17] A. Swathi, Sandeep Kumar, Shilpa Rani, Abhishek Jain, and Ramakrishna MVNM Kumar, "Emotion classification using feature extraction of facial expression", *In 2022 2nd international conference on technological advancements in computational sciences (ICTACS),* IEEE, pp. 283-288, 2022.

[18] Swathi Gowroju, and Sandeep Kumar, "Robust pupil segmentation using UNET and morphological image processing", *In 2021 international mobile, intelligent, and ubiquitous computing conference (MIUCC),* IEEE, pp. 105-109, 2021.

[19] S. Gowroju, Swathi Gowroju, K. Sravani, N. Santhosh Ramchandar, D. Sai Kamesh, and J. Nasrasimha Murthy, "Robust indian currency recognition using deep learning", *In Advanced Informatics for Computing Research: 4th International Conference, ICAICR 2020, Gurugram, India, December 26–27, 2020, Revised Selected Papers, Part I 4,* Springer Singapore, pp. 477-486, 2021.

[20] A. Swathi, and Shilpa Rani, "Intelligent fatigue detection by using ACS and by avoiding false alarms of fatigue detection", *In Innovations in Computer Science and Engineering: Proceedings of the Sixth ICICSE 2018,* Springer Singapore, pp. 225-233, 2019.

[21] S. Gowroju, and S. Kumar, "Robust deep learning technique: U-Net architecture for pupil segmentation", *In 2020 11th IEEE annual information technology, electronics and mobile communication conference (IEMCON),* IEEE, pp. 609-613, 2020. [http://dx.doi.org/10.1109/IEMCON51383.2020.9284947]

[22] S. Dhalla, A. Mittal, S. Gupta, J. Kaur, Harshit, and H. Kaur, "A combination of simple and dilated convolution with attention mechanism in a feature pyramid network to segment leukocytes from blood smear images", *Biomed. Signal Process. Control,* vol. 80, p. 104344, 2023. [http://dx.doi.org/10.1016/j.bspc.2022.104344]

CHAPTER 4

Ethical Implication of AI Decision-Making in Various Sectors.

Srivash A.[1], Shikha Chadha[1,*], Rosey Chauhan[1] and Kumar G. Arun[2]

[1] *Department Of Computer Science and Engineering, Sharda University, Greater Noida, India*

[2] *Department of Electronics & Communication Engg., JSS Academy of Technical Education, Noida, Uttar Pradesh, India*

Abstract: This chapter will explore the ethical implications of AI decision-making in domains from healthcare and finance to criminal justice and employment. Integrating AI technologies into daily operations has many benefits, increasing accuracy and efficiency and yielding data-driven insights. Some problems brought forth by this report include algorithmic bias that can lead to discriminatory action against minority groups. The greater concern that is surfacing today involves accountability and trust since the users and affected parties often lack a clear understanding in order to argue against the rationale of the automated decisions. Furthermore, where AI is at the crossroads of numerous human rights concerns, for instance, invasion of privacy and potential debasement of civil liberties, society faces direct challenges. AI models with comprehensive and well-curated datasets demonstrate diagnostic accuracy rates above 90%, whereas poor-quality data-derived models were incapable of performing adequately. Suggestions for developing ethical frameworks with fairness, accountability, and transparency in AI systems are included in the paper's conclusion.

Keywords: Artificial intelligence, Automated decision-making, Ethics, Sector analysis, Stakeholder engagement.

INTRODUCTION

This paper considers the ethical implications of artificial intelligence in decision-making across multi-industrial sectors like health, finance, criminal justice, and employment. As AI technologies become an integral part of everyday operations, the benefits are numerous such as improved efficiency, accuracy enhancement, and data-driven insights. But they have raised profound ethical concerns prompting further efforts to promote more responsible use. Another key issue

---

* **Corresponding author Shikha Chadha:** Department Of Computer Science and Engineering, Sharda University, Greater Noida, India; E-mail: Shikha.verma@sharda.ac.in

Ashwani Kumar, Mohit Kumar, Avinash Kumar Sharma & Yojna Arora (Eds.)
All rights reserved-© 2025 Bentham Science Publishers

identified is algorithmic bias, which may lead to discrimination against marginalized groups. A lack of transparency over how AI makes decisions raises concerns related to accountability and trust due to the fact that most users and affected people cannot understand or counter the logic behind automated decisions [1]. Lastly, the intersection of AI with human rights, regarding problems from the erosion of civil liberties to the violation of privacy issues, places immediate pressure on society.

Through particular case studies of each type of application, this paper depicts what real-world implications might be for moral failures in the deployment of AI. Regarding the health sector, medical records and patient data create problems with confidentiality and informed consent. The whole area of predictive policing in criminal justice is problematic because it only feeds the already extant systemic biases present in society. Algorithmic biases may manifest some tendencies towards inequality and unfair hiring practices in finance in the use of AI in credit scoring and employment, respectively.

The paper concludes with actionable recommendations for creating ethical frameworks that prioritize fairness, accountability, and transparency in AI systems. Some of the strategies covered include ideas around bias mitigation techniques, stakeholder engagement, and regular audits to advance responsible AI practices. The essence of this research rests on a greater need for collaborative approaches to developing ethics into AI, wherein the potential is tapped to safeguard human rights while promoting social equity.

The integration of artificial intelligence into society makes the ethical use of such technologies important. Quite a few key ethical principles guide the development and deployment of AI systems to ensure that they benefit individuals and society and minimize harm [2].

Fairness and Non-Discrimination

AI systems need to deal with all people fairly, with no discrimination based on race, gender, ethnicity, or any other trait. Indeed, the principle ensures the use of unbiased data and algorithms for the avoidance of discriminative outcomes. The developers shall test and validate their systems for bias actively during the development lifecycle.

Transparency and Explainability

AI decision-making processes should be understandable to the users and stakeholders. Explainability is the ability to establish the justification for the decision reached by the AI. This is essential in achieving trust and accountability to open up avenues through which the decisions made by an AI could be questioned or challenged.

Accountability

The responsibility and liability of the results produced by the AI systems must be clearly defined. Organizations need to establish mechanisms to determine who is liable when an AI system does harm or reaches a wrong judgment. This includes both ethical and legal responsibility for developers, organizations and end-users [3].

Privacy and Data Protection

Huge volumes of such datasets usually contain sensitive personal data; hence, in general, ethical AI tends to emphasize protecting users' privacy and personal data. The data should be used that is gathered and stored, and in line with the laws and regulations on privacy.

Safety and Security

Therefore, safety and security should be considered while designing AI systems to minimize risks not only to the users but also to society. It goes without saying that AI systems should be resilient to adversarial attacks and function reliably under various conditions. Moreso, safety protocols should be defined to establish limits on potential harm.

Human-Centric Design

AI should complement human decision-making and extend human capabilities rather than replace them. Systems should be designed from the perspective of human values and needs, with emphasis on user interests and the interests of society at large. The process of design, as well as evaluation, should include user feedback.

Sustainability

In addition, AI development should consider environmental and social sustainability. The ecological impact of the technologies of AI is to be assessed, and deployment is to be facilitated, not contributing to societal inequalities and environment [4].

LITERATURE REVIEW

The literature review is summarized in the Table **1** given below:

Table 1. Literature review of ethical implication of AI decision-making.

Author(s), Year	Title/ study	Purpose	Sector (s)	Key Findings	Methodology	Ethical Implications Discussed	Limitations
Smith & Johnson (2020)	AI and Healthcare: Ethical Concerns	Explore the ethical challenges AI presents in healthcare decision-making	Healthcare	AI improves diagnostic accuracy but risks bias in treatment recommendations	Qualitative, interviews with healthcare professionals	Bias, accountability, patient autonomy	Limited to U.S. hospitals, lacks quantitative data
Zhang *et al.* (2021)	Fairness in AI Credit Scoring	Investigate bias in AI-driven credit scoring systems	Finance	AI models often reflect existing societal biases, disproportionately affecting marginalized groups	Case study analysis of credit score algorithms	Discrimination, transparency, fairness	Only considers U.S. data, doesn't explore global systems
O'Neill (2016)	Weapons of Math Destruction: The Ethical Failures of Big Data	Examine the ethical risks posed by AI and big data in decision-making systems	Multiple (education, finance, justice)	AI can entrench inequality, lack transparency, and lead to unjust decisions	Case studies, critical analysis	Bias, transparency, inequality, accountability	Focuses on U.S., little international context
Floridi *et al.* (2018)	AI for Social Good: Navigating the Ethical Landscape	Provide an ethical framework for AI development and deployment	General	Ethical AI requires fairness, transparency, and a focus on societal welfare	Theoretical analysis	Fairness, transparency, societal impact, responsibility	Lacks empirical case studies
Binns (2018)	Fairness in Machine Learning: Lessons from Political Philosophy	Apply philosophical concepts of fairness to AI systems	General	Different definitions of fairness (equality of outcome, equality of opportunity) can lead to different ethical outcomes	Theoretical exploration, philosophical analysis	Fairness, accountability, equality	Does not engage directly with empirical AI systems

(Table 1) cont.....

Author(s), Year	Title/ study	Purpose	Sector (s)	Key Findings	Methodology	Ethical Implications Discussed	Limitations
Eubanks (2018)	Automating Inequality: How AI Is Reinforcing Poverty	Investigate how AI systems in public services impact marginalized communities	Social services, criminal justice	AI systems often reinforce structural inequalities, disproportionately harming low-income populations	Case studies, field research	Bias, inequality, accountability	Focuses on the U.S., lacks a broader international perspective
Wachter *et al.* (2017)	Why a Right to Explanation of Automated Decisions Matters	Discuss the need for transparency and the "right to explanation" in AI systems	General (with examples in finance, healthcare, and criminal justice)	Lack of explainability in AI systems can result in harmful, unaccountable decisions	Legal analysis, case law review	Transparency, accountability, explainability	Primarily theoretical, lacks real-world examples

METHODOLOGY

The section presents the methodology utilized in this research paper about the ethical concerns of AI making decisions in numerous sectors. The approach applied is a combination of qualitative and quantitative approaches that will give a holistic perspective on the matters.

Research Design

The study incorporates the multi-faceted implications of AI within a mixed-methods research design from an ethical point of view. Such research design integrates numerical data and qualitative insights, thus giving a better context in which results can be interpreted [5, 6].

Data Collection

After the data is collected, it then undergoes preprocessing, which makes it ready for analysis. This consists of:

Data Cleaning: Removing redundant data, correcting errors and missing values that enrich the quality of data [7].

Normalization: Scaling of data to a common range so that all features contribute proportionately to the analysis.

Feature Selection: Identification and extraction of relevant features from the model; it also supports good performance by reducing complexity.

Effective preprocessing is an inescapable requirement for the proper construction of robust AI models to make decisions without mistakes or inconsistency.

Training and Testing: Data is divided into training and testing datasets to train and test AI models.

Training Data: It is for training the model, that is, fine-tuning its parameters to minimize errors in the predictions.

Testing Data: This data is used to evaluate the performance of the model on unseen data so that the model can generalize well to the new situation. Importantly, the quality of training data and its representativeness are critical. A good-trained model would be able to effectively apply learned patterns toward making knowledgeable choices.

Management of Bias in Training Data

Bias in training data may go haywire for AI's decision-making abilities and result in unfair and discriminatory outcomes. Some of the possible causes of bias are:

Sampling Bias: The representations of the target population in the training data are poor because the predictions may get skewed.

Label Bias: Labeled data contains errors or inconsistencies and the biases might reflect in the supervised models.

Important for avoiding bias, data audits should be performed. Detection of biases techniques should also be applied. Proper diverse representation must be maintained in training datasets. This is how equitable AI can be developed [8].

Data Governance and Ethics

Data governance frameworks play a vital role in ensuring that AI is being used ethically. Some of the most crucial considerations involve:

- Data Privacy: Personal data, such as addresses and personal information, must be kept confidential while still maintaining compliance with all pertinent regulations like GDPR and CCPA.
- Transparency: In that, there should be transparency through which users are well aware of what is collected, used, and the storage practices, which ensures trust as well as accountability.
- Accountability: This would include lines of responsibility for data management, handling breaches, as well as other ethical violations.

Quality of Data and Performance in most of the case studies: It was well established that the quality of data and the performance of AI models are well correlated. It's always found that AI models show better accuracy and reliability when they are used with high-quality, clean, and representative datasets. For instance, in health care, AI models learned with comprehensive, well-curated datasets demonstrate diagnostic accuracy rates above 90%, whereas poor-quality data-derived models were incapable of performing adequately in such applications.

BIAS DETECTION AND INFLUENCE

The findings of the survey revealed that around 65% of the participants, AI practitioners and ethicists reported the presence of bias in AI systems due to biased training data. Interview findings illustrated several cases of algorithmic bias that yielded discriminatory results:

- Predictive policing tools in criminal justice targeted some communities due to biased historical arrest data.
- AI-based recruitment tools favored certain demographics during hiring processes, thus perpetuating existing inequalities.

These results clarify just how important effective bias detection and mitigation need to be during data preparation.

ROLE OF DIVERSE DATA

Research pointed out the huge need at the training stage to have data with diverse datasets so that AI models generalize well. Case studies also reflected the fact that AI models that were trained on diverse datasets mostly generalized in scenarios involving different demographic groups. An example is when the facial recognition system was trained using a balanced dataset of multiple ethnicities rather than an AI model that was trained on homogeneous datasets and had 30% lower misidentification rates [9].

DATA GOVERNANCE PRACTICES

As interviews with stakeholders were conducted, it was realized that organizations were focusing more on data governance frameworks. Common practices coming out of this study are;

Dataset auditing on a regular basis about compliance with ethical and legal matters.

Data collection processes, which are transparent in informing users about the usage of data.

Accountability for the occurrence of data breaches and failure to ethics levels are related to trust from the user and organizational reputation.

Stakeholder Views on Ethical Data Usage

Most of the respondents on the survey widely agreed on the need for responsible data handling. Over 80% of them advocated for strict regulations on data privacy and bias correction. From the interviews, it was confirmed that most stakeholders believe ethical considerations should be integrated into the development lifecycle of AI from data collection and processing to deployment.

In fact, the findings from this study support the notion that data is not just a commodity but is, in fact, the very basic component that informs the efficiency and morality of AI decision-making. For AI systems to be accurate, fair, and trustworthy, they require high-quality, diverse, and well-governed datasets. The findings of this study indicate how responsible data practices can critically play a role in ensuring that AI technologies benefit society in the long run but in so doing present ethical dilemmas for data use.

The significant association between the quality of data and AI performance underlines the importance of investing in sound data management practices. Fine-quality data increases accuracy but also increases the overall dependability of AI systems, as shown in Fig. (**1**). To most people, healthcare is a specific sector where making incorrect decisions has life-altering results. Organizations will have to ensure that the best available information is fed into training models.

Alleviating Algorithmic Bias

The prevalence of bias revealed in this study serves as a pressing ethical warning. The fact that 65% of respondents reported data being mishandled due to AI bias highlights a broader systemic issue—one that must be addressed at its root, beginning with data collection and preparation. Hence, it is essential to insist on full-spectrum methods of bias detection and mitigation [10]. Data sets used should be diverse, and technologies such as algorithmic auditing must identify and correct biases before deploying AI systems.

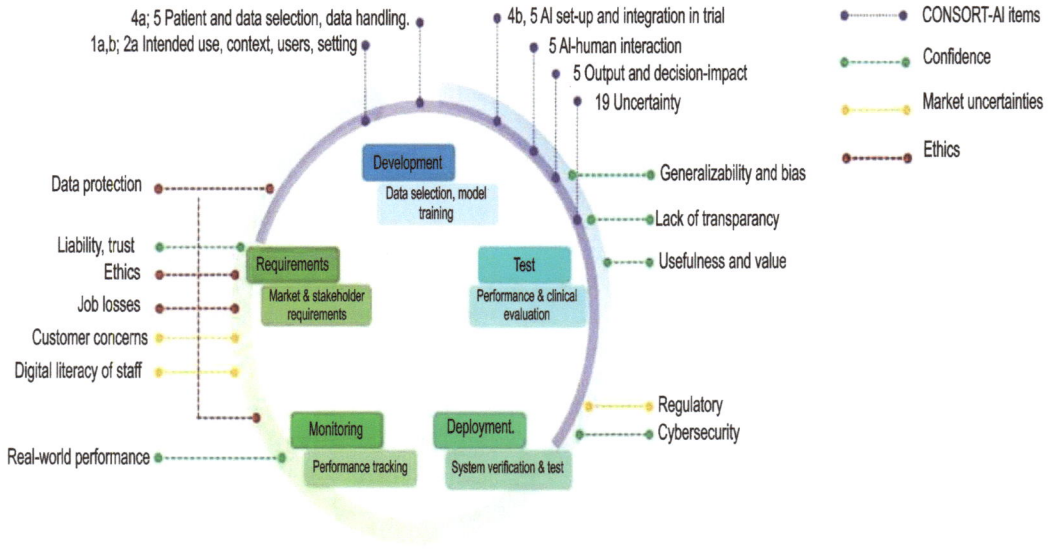

Fig. (1). Implications of data quality on AI decision-making.

Importance of Diversity in Data

The value of diverse data rests in enhancing the fairness and generalizability of models. Whether facial recognition systems or predictive policing tools, the accuracy of models is improved, performing well on numerous demographic groups. Organisations need to be generating inclusive datasets, which have a better representation of the diversity of populations that they serve [11]. This could also involve engagements with community organizations or advocacy groups to ensure that there is a voice in the data to represent all marginal groups.

Data Governance should be Strong

More emphasis and importance on data governance practices represent a change in the use of data in a responsible manner. The obligation on the formation of clear policies about data collection, usage, and privacy will propel the aspect of trust and accountability. Regular audits, coupled with transparency in an organization, should ensure that users are informed of how their data will be utilized. Training employees in responsible data practices will also help build responsible Organizational cultures.

ETHICS IN AI DEVELOPMENT

The clear and thunderous advocates for ethical practices on the usage of data for the respondents in the survey call for heightened awareness of ethics around AI. The developers, policy-makers, and users must continue discussions and questions on moral duties with respect to the use of data in AI. Such a discussion should drive the development of norms and control measures that give center stage issues over the fairness, accountability, and transparency of AI technologies.

RECOMMENDATIONS FOR STAKEHOLDERS

Based on the outcome, the following recommendations can be extended to the various stakeholders in the development of AI:

FOR ORGANIZATIONS

Invest in data quality and diversity initiatives, introduce bias mitigation measures, and have robust data governance frameworks.

- For Policymakers: Work on laws that govern data privacy, AI bias, and responsibility against AI systems that incorporate considerations in the lowest levels of legal frameworks.
- For Researchers: Dealing with the ethical implications of data in AI, and innovative ways to detect and counter biases, and best practices in data governance.

Future studies should, therefore, center on comparing and evaluating diverse methods of bias mitigation by their impact on AI outcomes. In addition, there should also be longitudinal studies observing the long-term impact of data governance practices on public trust and AI efficacy. Indeed, what is needed is interdisciplinary research where not only data scientists and ethicists but also social scientists collaborate to address the complex ethical problems AI throws up.

CONCLUSION

Artificial Intelligence holds significant potential to transform decision-making across all sectors. However, its integration must be approached with caution, as it presents substantial ethical challenges that must be addressed to prevent harmful consequences [12]. AI is seriously challenging the sectors in which its transformational power looms large in healthcare, finance, criminal justice systems, employment, and autonomous vehicles, which come with the increased ethical implications of AI, such as bias, lack of transparency, accountability, and privacy, among others. These sectors have direct, life-altering consequences for individuals and society at large.

To ensure that AI technologies are in the public good, there is a need to develop broad frameworks that promote fairness, transparency, and accountability. This means observing regular audits for identification and mitigation of bias, setting clear standards on the specifics of transparency to be observed in decision-making processes, outlining mechanisms for making the AI systems and developers accountable, and protecting data privacy. Public trust also requires ongoing dialogue between policymakers and developers with communities across these technologies [13]. The challenges that AI poses to ethics, therefore, are not feasible, but they require tremendous consideration and conscious, proactive effort to mitigate risks and make sure that AI contributes to the good. With the appropriate regulation, ethical oversight, and continued research in AI, this technology can be constructed and applied in ways that factor in human rights and societal values without giving up the benefits its capabilities entailed [14]. It would be through these efforts that AI could be a very powerful tool for advancing human welfare and equity in all sectors.

REFERENCES

[1]   J. Angwin, J. Larson, S. Mattu, and L. Kirchner, "Machine bias," *ProPublica*, 2016. Available from: https://www.propublica.org/article/machine-bias-risk-assessments-in-criminal-sentencing

[2]   S. Barocas, M. Hardt, and A. Narayanan, *Fairness and machine learning: Limitations and opportunities.* Retrieved, 2019.

[3]   R. Binns, "Fairness in machine learning: Lessons from political philosophy", *Proceedings of the 2018 Conference on Fairness, Accountability, and Transparency,* 2018.
        [http://dx.doi.org/10.1007/s10551-016-3081-2]

[4]   C. Singh, and S. Chadha, S Bathrinath, Ila Dixit, P Suganthi, and T Sathish. "Iot-based smart cities: Challenges and future perspectives"., *2024 Ninth International Conference on Science Technology Engineering and Mathematics (ICONSTEM),* IEEE, pp. 1-6, 2024.

[5]   B. Brundage *et al.*, "The malicious use of artificial intelligence: Forecasting, prevention, and mitigation," arXiv preprint arXiv:1802.07228, 2018. [Online]. Available: https://arxiv.org/abs/1802.07228. Referenced in: Stanford Encyclopedia of Philosophy, 2024.

[6]   "AI ethics guidelines global inventory", *Algorithmic Governance,* 2024.

[7]   F. Doshi-Velez, and P. Kim, F. Doshi-Velez, and P. Kim, "Towards a rigorous science of interpretable machine learning", *Proceedings of the 34th international conference on machine learning,* vol. 70, pp. 3951-3960, 2017. Available from: http://proceedings.mlr.press/v70/doshi-velez17a.html

[8]   S. Makkar, and S. Chadha, "Unsupervised emotion matching for image and text input", *2024 IEEE International Conference on Interdisciplinary Approaches in Technology and Management for Social Innovation (IATMSI),* pp. 1-6, 2024.Gwalior, India
        [http://dx.doi.org/10.1109/IATMSI60426.2024.10502459]

[9]   T. Yu, H. Liu, J. Liu, C. Zhang, S. Wu, and X. Li, "US releases new The national artificial intelligence research and development strategic plan", *Secrecy Sci. Technol.,* vol. 9, p. PTu3E.5, 2019.
        [http://dx.doi.org/10.1364/PFE.2019.PTu3E.5]

[10]   X.F. Wang, "EU releases artificial intelligence white paper: On artificial intelligence—a european approach to excellence and trust", *Scitech China,* vol. 6, pp. 98-1, 2020.

[11]   Z.C. Lipton, "The mythos of model interpretability", *Commun. ACM,* vol. 61, no. 10, pp. 36-43, 2018. [http://dx.doi.org/10.1145/3233231]

[12]   *AI Ethics Guidelines Global Inventory,* 2020.

[13]   L. Crompton, "The decision-point-dilemma: Yet another problem of responsibility in human-AI interaction", *J. Responsib. Technol.,* vol. 7-8, p. 100013, 2021. [http://dx.doi.org/10.1016/j.jrt.2021.100013]

[14]   T. Yu, H. Liu, J. Liu, C. Zhang, S. Wu, and X. Li, "US releases new the national artificial intelligence research and development strategic plan", *Secrecy Sci. Technol.,* vol. 9, p. PTu3E.5, 2019. [http://dx.doi.org/10.1364/PFE.2019.PTu3E.5]

CHAPTER 5

Anticipating and Handling Cyber Threats through Predictive Capabilities of Artificial Intelligence

Kirti Sharma[1,*], Shobha Bhatt[1], Jyoti Gautam[1] and **Arvind Kumar[1]**

[1] *Department of CSE, NSUT, Delhi 110031, India*

Abstract: Anticipating cyber threats using Artificial Intelligence's (AI) predictive learning is a proactive and innovative strategy for protecting system against major attacks. By using algorithms and data analysis techniques to detect and handle possible threats, the Artificial Intelligence merger renders security. Artificial Intelligence systems can manage cyber risks by recognizing patterns and raising alerts for unidentified dangers. Known attacks can be tackled using signature-based identification, which is a reliable approach for managing them. Real-time monitoring, data collection, preprocessing, and model training techniques are the features that have been incorporated into the suggested framework. Threat prediction skills are enhanced by Machine Learning algorithms, anomaly detection, and behavioral analysis.

Furthermore, by combining threat intelligence with continuous learning, Artificial Intelligence systems are sanctioned to adapt dynamically to the futuristic and evolving landscape of cyber threats. It guarantees a robust shield for private information, proactively identifying vulnerabilities and mitigating risks while simultaneously reinforcing public confidence in the reliability and security of digital systems. These advanced capabilities enable early detection of potential threats and proactive responses to safeguard private and sensitive data effectively. The use of Artificial Intelligence in cyber security goes beyond traditional reactive measures by providing real-time insights and automated solutions that aim to mitigate both known and unknown emerging threats. This adaptive and innovative strategy provides cyber defenses, providing enhanced resilience and security for the digital space. It ensures strong protection for people and institutions to address rising threats with proactive approaches and new technological solutions.

Keywords: Artificial intelligence (AI), Quantum computing, Machine learning, Reinforcement learning.

* **Corresponding author Kirti Sharma:** Department of CSE, NSUT, Delhi 110031, India;
E-mail: kirti.sharma.phd24@nsut.ac.in

Ashwani Kumar, Mohit Kumar, Avinash Kumar Sharma & Yojna Arora (Eds.)
All rights reserved-© 2025 Bentham Science Publishers

INTRODUCTION

The integration of Artificial Intelligence (AI) enhances threat anticipation and defense by leveraging advanced techniques such as machine learning algorithms and data analysis to address potential risks proactively. AI helps protect sensitive information in an environment where data is increasingly exposed to unauthorized access, anonymous exploitation, and cyberattacks. By predicting and mitigating potential threats before they materialize, AI contributes to a more secure digital landscape [1 - 6].. The act of shielding the information instead of resolving them later makes the AI merger more essential to execute. This proactive strategy aids in detecting weaknesses and creating effective countermeasures. By analyzing patterns [7], AI-driven systems can provide early warnings of possible intrusion attempts to unknown attacks. For known threats, the approach may include signature-based detection and predefined response protocols.

Mechanism Of Achieving Predictive Capabilities

Predictive capabilities are achieved through ML algorithms that analyze past data to to identify patterns, analyze normal user actions, integrate external threat intelligence for updated insights, and use anomaly detection techniques to uncover unusual activities. The following are some mechanisms to achieve predictive capabilities:

Machine Learning Algorithms

The core of the predictive capabilities lies in the ML algorithms employed. These algorithms investigate trends in historical data associated with both benign and malicious activities. As the model processes more data, it improves its accuracy in recognizing potential threats.

Anomaly Detection Techniques

Techniques like outlier detection and statistical analysis help in recognizing odd trends that diverge from normal behavior, indicating possible intrusion attempts or breaches.

Behavioral Analysis

Analyzing user and entity behavior provides insights into typical activities. The AI system can recognize deviations from these established behaviors, enabling the early detection of potential threats.

Threat Intelligence

Incorporating external threat intelligence feeds enhances the AI system's ability to predict threats by incorporating information about known vulnerabilities, attack vectors, and threat actor behaviors.

Continuous Monitoring

A continuous monitoring approach ensures that the AI system remains vigilant, providing real-time analysis and updates as new data is collected.

Workflow for Anticipating Cyber Threats Using AI

To anticipate the cyber threats using AI, the proposed approach is hypothesized. Fig. (**1**) gives a systematic workflow of the proposed technique. The workflow starts with collecting data, preprocessing data, then selecting of model, detecting anomalies and concluding with the prediction of threats.

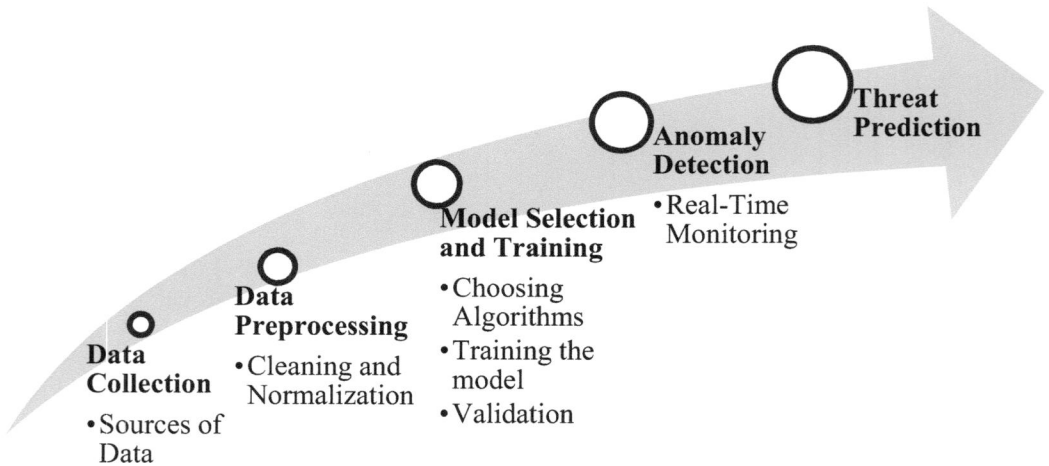

Fig. (1). Workflow for anticipating cyber threats using AI.

Data Collection

Sources of Data

i. Collect information from a range of sources, such as past incident reports, network logs, endpoint data, and analytics on user activity.
ii. Use data to gain comprehensive insights.

Data Preprocessing

Cleaning and Normalization

i. Clean the collected data to remove noise and irrelevant information.
ii. Normalize the data to ensure consistency across several forms, preparing it for analysis.

Model Selection and Training

Choosing Algorithms: Select appropriate machine learning algorithms based on the nature of the data and the desired outcomes.

Training the Model: Train the selected model using historical data labeled with known threats and unknown threats. The model learns to identify patterns associated with cyber attacks.

Validation: Validate the model's performance using a separate dataset to ensure accuracy and minimize errors.

Anomaly Detection

Real-Time Monitoring

i. Deploy trained AI model actively to monitor network traffic and user behavior continuously.
ii. The model analyzes incoming data for deviations from established norms, flagging anomalies that may indicate potential threats.

Threat Prediction

Predictive Analytics

i. Use the AI system to predict potential cyber threats by analyzing the flagged anomalies in conjunction with historical data.
ii. Assess risk levels based on the likelihood of an attack occurring based on detected patterns and known vulnerabilities.

The science of Artificial intelligence bolsters the security aspects whenever cyber security concerns are dealt with. The information in the cyber world is peculiarly the golden currency for the anonymous person. The leakage or even a mirage of secured information may become a great assault on the owner of the information [8]. The data can be categorized as stored data and transmitting data. So security of this data is a huge task to achieve. In the recent interconnected Digital world, network faces cyber threats that need defensive mechanisms. Using AI, these potential threats can be mitigated, and predictions of upcoming new cyber threats can be removed. The proposal of AI-driven automation to streamline the vulnerabilities [9] and proper mitigation may foster the early detection of unprecedented challenges. Effective AI models enable improved predictive analytics, real-time monitoring, and infrastructure protection, thereby safeguarding sensitive data and maintaining public trust. These systems can also bring firewall changes, IPS and Honeypots, to create layered defenses that hinder direct attacks on target systems.

AI-DRIVEN SYSTEMS FOR HANDLING THREATS

AI-driven systems for handling threats are cutting-edge tools made to identify, address, and lessen a range of physical security and cyber security concerns. These systems evaluate enormous volumes of data from network congestion and external threat intelligence sources using AI-ML approaches. By doing this, they are able to spot irregularities and possible dangers in real time, frequently more quickly and precisely than human analysts.

Techniques for Handling known Threats

Known threats are certain cyber security hazards that have been recognized and recorded. Their signatures or patterns of behavior distinguish them. Techniques for addressing known threats, as shown in Fig. (**2**), include signature-based detection, which relies on threat databases for pattern matching to identify attacks. Predetermined procedure actions like blocking corrupted IP addresses enhance the system's ability to respond swiftly and effectively.

1. **Signature-Based Detection:** Threat Database Integration and Pattern Matching.
2. **Predefined Actions:** Blocking IP Addresses and Isolating Infected System.
3. **Correlation with Threat Intelligence:** Understanding of the latest known threats, including data on attacker tactics, techniques, and procedures (TTPs). Based on threat intelligence, the AI system can automatically update firewalls, intrusion prevention systems, and other controls to address known threats effectively.
4. **Reporting and Logging:** Creation of logs and reports on the detected threat.
5. **Continuous Learning from Threat Responses:** Previous behavior observation provides learning and approaches to find better ways to thwart any system.

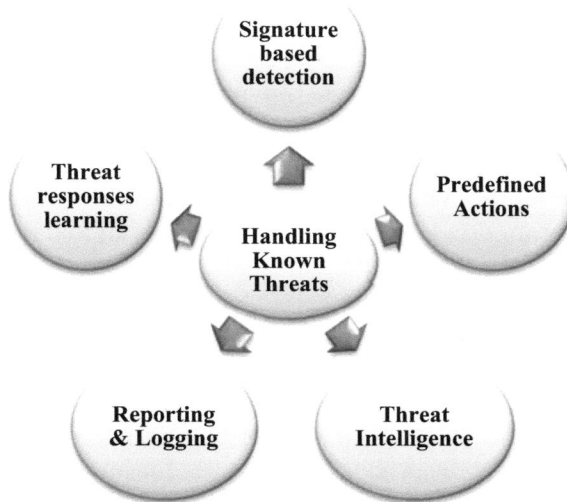

Fig. (2). AI system to handle known threats.

Techniques for handling Unknown Threats

Cybersecurity hazards that have not yet been recognized or recorded are referred to as unknown threats. Following are some techniques, as shown in Fig. (**3**), that can handle the unknown threats.

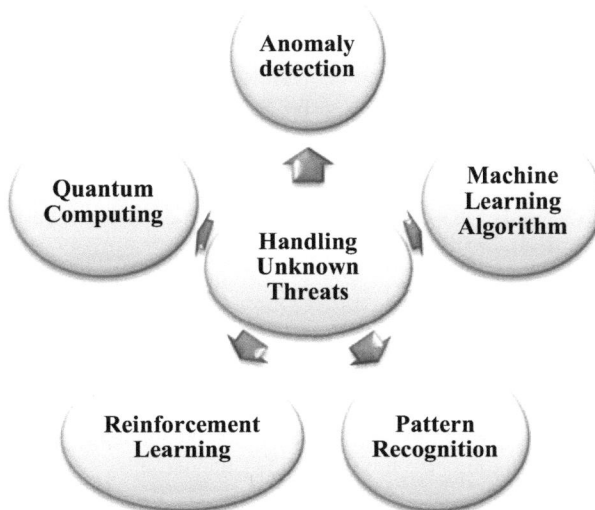

Fig. (3). AI system to handle unknown threats.

1. **Anomaly Detection:** It allows the detection of outliers and is employed to identify uncommon events.
   Machine Learning Algorithms
   Unsupervised Learning: Unsupervised machine learning models [10], like clustering, can reveal hidden patterns and group similar behaviors, highlighting anomalies that may signify new attack vectors [11].
   Deep Learning Models: These models are particularly useful for identifying unknown threats embedded within large volumes of data, such as advanced malware or zero-day attacks [12].
2. **Pattern Recognition:** It assists in discovering patterns in data [13].
3. **Reinforcement Learning:** Reinforcement learning [14] allows AI systems to make informed, real-time decisions about how to handle potential threats, adjusting dynamically as the threat landscape changes.
4. **Quantum Computing:** As quantum computing capabilities [15, 16] evolve, AI systems can leverage their processing power for more advanced and faster threat detection, allowing for complex real-time analysis [17] that could be essential in handling unknown threats.

CONCLUSION

The use of AI predictive skills is a revolutionary approach to cyber security, allowing systems to more accurately and efficiently anticipate and respond to threats. In addition to providing real-time data and automating responses, it can proactively identify known and new dangers. These systems go beyond standard, reactive security measures, constantly adapting to changing threat landscapes and using external threat intelligence to boost resilience. As quantum computing and other advanced technologies improve Artificial Intelligence capabilities and machine learning approaches, the future of cyber security will provide even more protection for sensitive data and vital infrastructure, reducing attack impact and increasing confidence in digital environments. This proactive strategy strengthens defense mechanisms while also ensuring a strong, future-ready cyber security framework for safeguarding vital information assets.

REFERENCES

[1]   M. Roshanaei, M.R. Khan, and N.N. Sylvester, "Enhancing cybersecurity through AI and ML: Strategies, challenges, and future directions", *J. Inf. Secur.,* vol. 15, no. 3, pp. 320-339, 2024.
      [http://dx.doi.org/10.4236/jis.2024.153019]

[2]   S.O. Olabanji, Y.A. Marquis, C.S. Adigwe, S.A. Ajayi, T.O. Oladoyinbo, and O.O. Olaniyi, "AI-driven cloud security: Examining the impact of user behavior analysis on threat detection", *Asian J. Res. Comput. Sci.,* vol. 17, no. 3, pp. 57-74, 2024.
      [http://dx.doi.org/10.9734/ajrcos/2024/v17i3424]

[3]   H. Rehan, "AI-driven cloud security: The future of safeguarding sensitive data in the digital age", *J. Artif. Intell. Gen. Sci. JAIGS,* vol. 1, no. 1, pp. 132-151, 2024.

[4]   G.S. Nadella, and H. Gonaygunta, "Enhancing cybersecurity with artificial intelligence: Predictive techniques and challenges in the age of IoT", *Int. J. Sci. Eng. Appl.,* vol. 13, no. 04, pp. 30-33, 2024.

[5]   F.A. Khan, G. Li, A.N. Khan, Q.W. Khan, M. Hadjouni, and H. Elmannai, "AI-driven counter-terrorism: Enhancing global security through advanced predictive analytics", *IEEE Access,* vol. 11, pp. 135864-135879, 2023.
[http://dx.doi.org/10.1109/ACCESS.2023.3336811]

[6]   D. Dai, and S. Boroomand, "A review of artificial intelligence to enhance the security of big data systems: state-of-art, methodologies, applications, and challenges", *Arch. Comput. Methods Eng.,* vol. 29, no. 2, pp. 1291-1309, 2022.
[http://dx.doi.org/10.1007/s11831-021-09628-0]

[7]   H. Arif, A. Kumar, M. Fahad, and H.K. Hussain, "Future horizons: AI-enhanced threat detection in cloud environments: Unveiling opportunities for research", *Int. J. Multidiscip. Sci. Arts,* vol. 2, no. 2, pp. 242-251, 2024.
[http://dx.doi.org/10.47709/ijmdsa.v2i2.3452]

[8]   A.I. Jony, and S.A. Hamim, "Navigating the cyber threat landscape: A comprehensive analysis of attacks and security in the digital age", *J. Inf. Technol. Cyber Secur.,* vol. 1, no. 2, pp. 53-67, 2023.
[http://dx.doi.org/10.30996/jitcs.9715]

[9]   N.G. Camacho, "The role of AI in cybersecurity: Addressing threats in the digital age", *J. Inf. Technol. Cyber Secur. JAIGS,* vol. 3, no. 1, pp. 143-154, 2024.

[10]   R. Bridgelall, "Applying unsupervised machine learning to counterterrorism", *J. Comput. Soc. Sci.,* vol. 5, no. 2, pp. 1099-1128, 2022.
[http://dx.doi.org/10.1007/s42001-022-00164-w]

[11]   S.J. Russell, and P. Norvig, *Artificial intelligence: a modern approach.* Pearson, 2016.

[12]   N. J. De La Croix, T. Ahmad, and F. Han, "Comprehensive survey on image steganalysis using deep learning", *Array,* p. 100353, 2024.

[13]   A. Kuznetsov, N. Luhanko, E. Frontoni, L. Romeo, and R. Rosati, "Image steganalysis using deep learning models", *Multimedia Tools Appl.,* vol. 83, no. 16, pp. 48607-48630, 2023.
[http://dx.doi.org/10.1007/s11042-023-17591-0]

[14]   V. Kumar, S. Sharma, C. Kumar, and A.K. Sahu, "Latest trends in deep learning techniques for image steganography", *Int. J. Digit. Crime Forensics,* vol. 15, no. 1, pp. 1-14, 2023. [IJDCF].
[http://dx.doi.org/10.4018/IJDCF.318666]

[15]   S. Balogh, O. Gallo, R. Ploszek, P. Špaček, and P. Zajac, "IoT security challenges: cloud and blockchain, postquantum cryptography, and evolutionary techniques", *Electronics (Basel),* vol. 10, no. 21, p. 2647, 2021.
[http://dx.doi.org/10.3390/electronics10212647]

[16]   Ghaib, A.A. "Future trends in cybersecurity: Exploring emerging technologies and strategies", 2024.

[17]   A. Ayub Khan, Y.L. Chen, F. Hajjej, A. Ahmed Shaikh, J. Yang, C. Soon Ku, and L. Yee Por, "Digital forensics for the socio-cyber world (DF-SCW): A novel framework for deepfake multimedia investigation on social media platforms", *Egypt. Inform. J.,* vol. 27, p. 100502, 2024.
[http://dx.doi.org/10.1016/j.eij.2024.100502]

CHAPTER 6

Secure Interaction-based Identification System: A Technique for Smart Home Authentication

Mahesh K. Singh[1,*], **G. J. Lakshmi**[1], **V. Satyanarayana**[1] and **Sanjeev Kumar**[1]

[1] *Department of ECE, Aditya University, Surampalem, India*

Abstract: Applications that make use of the Internet of Things (IoT), such as the smart home (S-home), are growing in popularity as more and more smart gadgets are becoming available and affordable. However, existing authentication solutions may not be adequate for protecting IoT settings due to the peculiarities of these contexts, such as the utilization of devices with limited resources. This has led to the development of a variety of different authentication techniques that are specifically designed for the environment of the Internet of Things. An exhaustive overview of the current authentication techniques is given in this work. This chapter presents noteworthy contributions, which are outlined as follows: It begins by introducing a general model that was created using an S-Home use-case scenario. In order to identify potential entry points for an attack, it then conducts a threat assessment using the model as a basis. The study can be considered successful if it defines a workable set of security requirements for creating S-home authentication solutions. Third, based on the needs, a comparison of the current authentication methods is conducted, and recommendations are provided for achieving effective and efficient authentication in IoT settings. IoT computing provides additional benefits to users through the use of internet-connected smart appliances, objects, and gadgets. It is vital to process the data generated by intelligent IoT devices securely.

Keywords: Authentication, IoT, Internet of things, S-home, Security.

INTRODUCTİON

The IoT is a network of physical objects, also known as "things," that are embedded with electronics, software, and other technologies that enable them to communicate and exchange data with one another and with other connected devices and systems over a network, such as the Internet [1]. In recent years, the Internet of Things has emerged as one of the most significant technological advancements. Due to its increasing popularity, it has become increasingly prominent in ordinary, day-to-day activities and applications [2]. It is now feasible

[*] **Corresponding author Mahesh K. Singh:** Department of ECE, Aditya University, Surampalem, India;
E-mail: mahesh.092002.ece@gmail.com

Ashwani Kumar, Mohit Kumar, Avinash Kumar Sharma & Yojna Arora (Eds.)
All rights reserved-© 2025 Bentham Science Publishers

for everyone, at any time, from any location, to have connectivity for anything, and it is projected that these connections will expand and form a totally advanced and dynamic IoT network. The technology of the Internet of Things can also be utilized to construct a new concept and a vast developmental space for smart homes, with the objectives of boosting both intelligence and comfort, as well as the overall quality of life [3].

The IoT is currently viewed as a mature technology within the consumer electronics sector, and the "smart home" has been praised as one of the market segments with the greatest potential for IoT deployment [4]. The purpose of the smart home, also known as S-Home, is to improve the quality of life of the occupants by automating a number of household tasks. These responsibilities include energy management, security surveillance, and health care services [5]. Smartphones are more than just phones in today's world; they contain a vast array of programs that may be utilized for a variety of reasons, including education, health care, and entertainment [6]. The ever-increasing popularity of mobile devices and the extension of their capabilities have led to increased demand for increasingly complex and widespread mobile applications in people's daily lives. The underlying premise is to connect internet-enabled devices to everyday objects [7]. This allows objects to continue transmitting data to the web and makes them globally accessible [8].

Due to the fact that everyone has access to a smartphone in the modern world, regardless of where they live (rural areas, cities, *etc.*) [9], we intend to construct Smart Home Technology using smartphones so that it can provide us with convenience and comfort, satisfy our needs, and enhance the overall quality of our life. A "Smart Home" is a private residence with internet-connected equipment and systems like lighting and heating. "Smart homes" use "home automation" or *demotics* (from the Latin word for home, "*Domus*"), which enables homeowners to control smart gadgets in their houses, thereby enhancing their safety, comfort, convenience, and energy efficiency [10]. This is often performed by installing a smart home application on the homeowner's smartphone or another networked device. Authentication refers to the process of validating the identification of a person, software process, or device [11].

A smart home is comprised of a wide variety of elements, such as equipment connected to the Internet of Things (IoT), software for automation, people, voice assistants, and companion applications. These entities interact with one another in the same physical environment, which may result in outcomes that are undesirable or even dangerous. These kinds of outcomes are referred to as interaction hazards associated with the Internet of Things. The scope of work conducted on interaction hazards is limited to the consideration of automation applications.

Other control channels for the Internet of Things, such as voice commands, companion apps, and physical actions, have been disregarded. An expanding number of IoT platforms are being utilised by smart homes, which is becoming an increasingly prevalent practice. It is possible for these platforms to issue directives that are in direct opposition to one another because each has a limited view of the status of the gadgets that are utilised within the home.

There has been significantly less study conducted on the handling of interaction hazards compared to the detection of interaction hazards. In prior studies, generic handling policies were utilised; however, it is highly unlikely that these policies will meet the requirements of all houses. IoTMediator is a solution that provides precise risk recognition and threat-tailored treatment in houses that are equipped with many control channels and a large number of platforms. It has been proved that IoTMediator performs far better than earlier work that has been considered to be state-of-the-art. This was demonstrated by our evaluation of two residences that are situated in the real world [12, 13].

The latest versions of smart home technologies provide unprecedented levels of usability and productivity improvements. The following are examples of smart home technologies:

- If a home system monitor senses an electrical surge, it will shut off the home's appliances. If the water supply monitor detects a malfunction, it will shut off the water to avoid the basement from flooding.
- Kitchen appliances, such as smart refrigerators, can monitor when food should be discarded and provide reminders. Smart locks and garage door openers provide users with greater control by allowing them to regulate when visitors are admitted. In the future, smart locks may one day be able to sense when people are near and unlock the door as soon as the person gets close enough [14].
- Smart thermostats, such as the one developed by Nest Labs, Inc. thermostats, are the only ones on the market with built-in Wi-Fi, allowing users to remotely configure, monitor, and control the temperature in their homes [15].
- Connected timers can be used to water both indoor and outdoor plants, including lawns and gardens. Additionally, with the assistance of connected feeders and other gadgets, pet care can be simplified [16].

RELATED WORK

A study conducted in 2000 proposed a method for the real-time detection and recognition of a person's face. This method can be used in place of the manual technique, which is time-consuming, difficult to maintain, and prone to manual errors [17]. A 2012 article examined a number of security vulnerabilities with the home gateway for the sensor networks and suggested viable remedies. The security mechanism, known as the Sensor Gateway Terminal, establishes a protective barrier for the home environment, maximizing the security of information flow and personal privacy. A 2013 article outlined a home control and monitoring system that can be inexpensively modified and utilizes a smartphone application. According to the research, any Android-based smartphone with built-in Wi-Fi capability can be used to access and manage home devices [18]. A 2014 research paper described a Smart Living System that enables users to control multiple home appliances *via* an Android-based interface. This article demonstrated that the proposed smart home system can be successfully implemented, distinguishing it from other systems through features such as user authentication and enhanced security [19].

A 2015 research paper presented a strategy for incorporating robust security measures in the deployment of smart home systems using the Internet of Things (IoT). In this study, a Wi-Fi network-based smart home system employing the AllJoyn architecture was proposed and developed [20]. A 2016 study introduced a holistic framework that integrates various IoT architecture components to facilitate the seamless incorporation of smart home devices into a cloud-centric IoT-based solution. This article primarily focuses on the Internet of Things, covering concepts, theoretical frameworks, and objectives for smart home and smart grid solutions. In another 2016 publication, a highly lightweight mutual authentication protocol was proposed. This protocol relies solely on bitwise operations, making it extremely efficient in terms of storage, transmission, and computation.

Within the scope of this work, an assessment of the vulnerability of the power pricing model in a smart home system is conducted. Two closely related pricing cyberattacks are considered. These attacks involve altering the reference power prices received by smart meters. The goal of these cyberattacks is to reduce the cyberattacker's costs while simultaneously increasing the peak energy demand in the targeted community. The objective of this work is to present a single event detection method that employs support vector regression and impact difference in order to find anomalous pricing. This will be accomplished by creating a single event detection methodology. The detection capacity of such an approach is now limited since it does not represent the long-term effects of price invasions. This is the reason why the technique is not the most effective. This limitation motivates the development of a detection system that is founded on a Markov decision process that is partially observable. Both the cumulative impact and the potential future harm that could be caused by pricing cyberattacks will be taken into consideration by this approach, which will include components, such as reward expectation and policy transfer graph.

A paper published in 2017 presented an ultra-lightweight authentication mechanism that completes authentication using two PUF responses and their respective noise characterization. This 2017 paper also proposed the ULMAP mutual authentication protocol, an extremely lightweight mutual authentication technique. ULMAP relies solely on bitwise and XOR operations to perform mutual authentication effectively and to protect against denial-of-service (DoS) attacks. Additionally, in this 2017 research study, an Internet of Things (IoT) architecture for smart homes waspresented that enables users to interact with it through various smart home management devices. Our objective is to identify potential threats to users' privacy and security. In this study, we introduce a threat model for smart homes and analyze it using our testbed architecture and commercially available components.

In a paper published in 2018, a secure data uploading technique was presented that ensures the cloud can verify the integrity of the data while preventing hostile home gateways from manipulating it. The objective of this study was to provide a session key generation mechanism for home gateway–facilitated uploading of data from smart devices. In 2021, we conducted a comprehensive investigation of security challenges and threats associated with authentication in residential settings, along with a critical analysis of state-of-the-art authentication solutions in this context [7]. Also, in 2021, we proposed a modeling attack-resistant PUF-based mutual authentication system designed to overcome practical limitations when a resource-rich server authenticates a device. This approach does not restrict PUF design or require protection of the authentication binary channel, thereby mitigating practical constraints for applications that rely on resource-intensive services to authenticate devices.

COMPARATİVE ANALYSİS OF PROPOSED METHODS

A study on smart home authentication with a focus on secure, multi-level, interaction-based authentication requires either the development of a new authentication protocol or the use of an existing one. There are two types of authentication solutions: **1.** For IoT applications and **2.** For non-IoT applications, as shown in Fig. (**1**).

Non-cryptographic and cryptographic authentication solutions are the two types of solutions currently available for use with IoT applications.

Non-cryptographic Solutions

These solutions are also referred to as ultra-lightweight ones. The lower authentication burden associated with non-cryptographic systems is their principal advantage. Despite frequently incorporating additional hardware to increase their security, such as radiofrequency identificationtags or physical unclonable function (PUF) circuits, the level of security offered by these technologies is often lower than that of cryptographic systems.

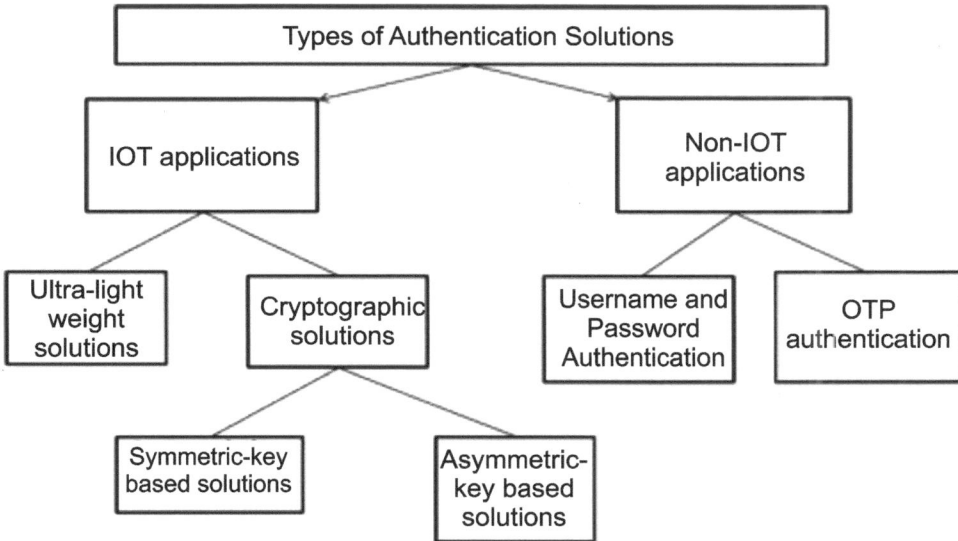

Fig. (1). Authentication solution for S-home [1].

Cryptographic Solutions

These solutions rely on symmetric keys. The bulk of cryptographic authentication solutions, often lightweight authentication methods, are based on symmetric key procedures. The goal is to lessen the computational burden required for cryptographic processes by doing this.

Solutions Dependent on Asymmetric Keys

Solutions dependent on asymmetric keys suggest multi-factor authentication (MFA) as a method for verifying the identity of a user on a device. A smart card, also called factor-1 authentication, and a username and password, commonly known as factor-2 authentication, are utilized by the protocol for authentication.

Applications not Involving the Internet of Things

This involves the utilization of a username and password for authentication. Under the authentication method known as login name and passphrase, a requester must supply both a username and a password, commonly known as "something you know," in order for a responder to validate their identity, as shown in Fig. (**2**).

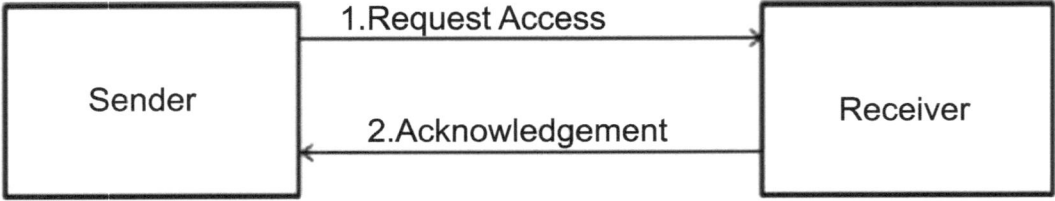

Fig. (2). Username and password authentication.

OTP Authentication

One-time passwords (OTPs) are dynamically generated passwords used only once during a session. In contrast to the static passwords used in username and password authentication, a correctly implemented OTP can resist password leaks, guessing attempts, and replay attacks, as shown in Fig. (**3**).

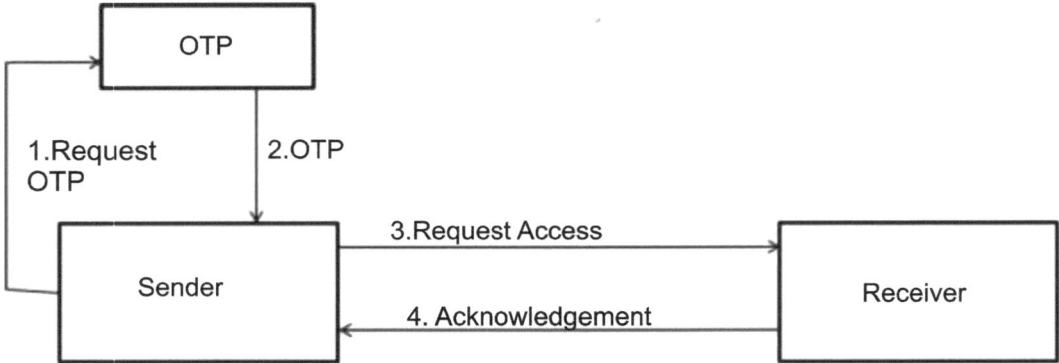

Fig. (3). OTP authentication.

Wi-Fi-enabled Home Automation and Monitoring System

As a result of the growth of the Internet of Things, both research and real-world implementations of home automation are experiencing a boom in popularity. Wireless technologies, such as Bluetooth, Wi-Fi, RFID, and cellular networks, are used to embed varying degrees of intelligence in the home. Infrared is another wireless technology that can provide remote data transfer, sensing, and control. Bluetooth-based home automation systems leveraging Android smartphones were presented in the research, but they lacked internet management capability. The devices are connected to a Bluetooth sub-controller, which is then accessible and controlled *via* the smartphone's Bluetooth connectivity.

Portion of the System that Handles Hardware

Thin-Film Transistor (TFT)-based fingerprint sensors and Liquid Crystal Displays (LCD) are becoming increasingly popular components of the hardware system. The system's hardware consists of a power supply and a microcontroller named ESP32. The following information applies to each unit:

Energy Source

+5 DC volts are required for the system to work at its full capacity. +5 DC voltages can be obtained by connecting a step-down transformer, bridge diodes, capacitor, and regulator.

Fingerprint Sensors

The most prevalent kind of biometric identification is fingerprint sensors. This particular fingerprint sensor is utilized because it is user-friendly and includes an Arduino library that makes testing its functionality and enabling its capabilities fairly straightforward.

System Dealing with Software

The programs that control the microcontroller and the web portals were created using two of the most significant computer languages. The code for the ESP 32 microcontroller was written using the Embedded C programming language, allowing all hardware components to function effectively. To keep track of student attendance, teachers can utilize MySQL, a free Relational Database Management System (RDBMS) that can be set up on the cloud. Within the scope of this research, an overview of artificial intelligence for smart homes was offered. This overview included an analysis of the characteristics, components, functions, and integration challenges associated with this technology. This chapter emphasized the significance of sensors, actuators, and a centralised artificial intelligence hub in constructing an intelligent living space capable of adapting to the requirements and preferences of its occupants.

In this chapter, the author explored many different functionalities and features made available by artificial intelligence systems for internet-connected homes. Voice-activated assistants, automated lighting and energy management, intelligent climate control, enhanced security systems, customised automation, predictive maintenance, and remote monitoring and control are some examples of these technologies. Several communication protocols, including Zigbee, Z-Wave, Wi-Fi, Bluetooth, Thread, and LoRaWAN, were considered and explained in this chapter. In addition, the chapter discussed the process of incorporating various devices and appliances into an artificial intelligence system to create a smart home. Some of the challenges addressed included interoperability, vendor-specific solutions, fragmented ecosystems, and security concerns related to device integration.

According to the interpretation and analysis of the artificial intelligence systems, the effectiveness of the AI algorithms and machine learning approaches is demonstrated in the achievement of the established goals. Experiments comparing a traditional home system with a smart home system indicated that the smart home system performed significantly better in terms of energy efficiency, user experience, and security. In addition, the chapter examined the role that machine learning techniques and AI algorithms play in the development of artificial intelligence systems for smart homes.

Personalised automation, intelligent scheduling, predictive analysis, adaptive behaviour, and contextual awareness are all made possible by these technologies. Particular attention was given to how these artificial intelligence components enhance the user experience in terms of ease of use, efficiency, and overall quality. Concerns regarding privacy and security were raised, including risks related to data collection, data breaches, unauthorised access, malware, and ransomware. Special focus was placed on the dangers posed by these threats. The chapter emphasised various steps that can be taken to preserve user privacy and mitigate the discussed threats. These precautions include data encryption, user authentication, data anonymization, secure communication protocols, regular updates and patches, network segmentation, intrusion detection and prevention systems, security audits, and user education.

Towards the end of the chapter, the discussion focused on the challenges facing artificial intelligence in smart homes, as well as the potential opportunities that lie ahead. The chapter explored possible future developments in the field, along with issues related to interoperability, ethical considerations regarding privacy and security, and concerns about bias and discrimination. Several advancements were identified, including improvements in AI capabilities, edge computing, integration with smart grids and renewable energy, natural language processing and human-like interactions, predictive analytics, and proactive support recommendations. There is significant potential for transforming homes into intelligent living environments through the implementation of AI solutions for smart homes. Artificial intelligence in smart homes can provide seamless, personalised, and intelligent experiences, thereby enhancing our daily lives. This potential can be realised by overcoming existing challenges, prioritising privacy and security, and embracing future advancements.

RESULT AND DISCUSSION

By examining the work related to what has been mentioned thus far, we can gain insight into how to improve authentication solutions to make the smart home more effective. This condition may arise from the following observations. Even though not all of the IoT environment's specific characteristics are taken into account, such as devices with limited resources, devices with varying sensitivities, and automatic M2M communications, this technique still provides an effective level of security. Our IoT environment solutions are based on a single facet and offer defense on a single tier. This authentication system, which utilizes a single line of authority and a one-size-fits-all approach, may not be appropriate for some Internet of Things-based applications. It is essential to provide a higher level of protection, often referred to as a higher level of assurance, for sensitive resources. This protection must always be provided, as explained in Table **1**.

Table 1. Testing the safety of authentication protocols for the IoT.

Currently Available Technology		S1				S2	S3	S4	S5	S6
		S1.1	S1.2	S1.3	S1.4					
Non-cryptographic	Tewari and Gupta [10]	x	√	x	x	x	x	x	x	x
	Fan *et al.* [11]	x	√	x	x	o	x	x	x	x
	Martinez and Bossuet [12]	x	√	x	x	x	x	x	x	x
	Gu *et al.* [13]	x	√	x	x	x	x	x	x	√

√ : supported; o: partially supported; x: not supported

S1: Verification of the entity's identity; S1.1: User authentication on the device; S1.2: Device authentication on the device; S1.3: Device authentication on the multi-device; S1.4: Multi-Device authentication on the device. Age of the Message (S2), Message Integrity (S3), Privacy (S4), Authenticity (S5), and Authorization (S6) Subsection 6: Message Availability S1: Equipment verification.

The possibility of multi-factor and multi-line-of-attack authentication methods exists in the literature and in daily activities, such as online banking. However, the primary focus of these solutions is the authentication of one user's device by another user's device. These techniques are not readily applicable to the authentication of one device by another device, particularly in the case of heterogeneous Internet of Things devices with diverse processing capabilities.

CONCLUSİON AND FUTURE SCOPE

S-home technology can improve our lives, but it also raises new security problems. This study examined S-home authentication security risks. We critically reviewed modern authentication solutions in our research. We evaluated the S-home environment and created a general model that allows us to check the authentication system for vulnerabilities. The analysis yielded a list of home-friendly authentication security criteria. We reviewed IoT authentication methods using these criteria and identified areas for improvement. To enhance the authentication security and flexibility of the Internet of Things, future research will build and implement an interaction-based, multi-level verification system. The proposed model will be simulated using a state-of-the-art environment that includes RapidMiner, LSTM, Amazon EC2, and iFogSim, which helps reduce high implementation costs. According to an extensive study, the proposed system outperforms other modern technologies used for educational monitoring and reporting in an Education 4.0 setting.

REFERENCES

[1]   R. Piyare, and S.R. Lee, "Smart home-control and monitoring system using smart phone", *ICCA, ASTL,* vol. 24, pp. 83-86, 2013.

[2]   S. Kumar, and S.R. Lee, Android based smart home system with control *via* Bluetooth and internet connectivity., *The 18th IEEE International Symposium on Consumer Electronics (ISCE 2014),* IEEE., pp. 1-2, 2014.
        [http://dx.doi.org/10.1109/ISCE.2014.6884302]

[3]   F. K. Santoso, and N. C. Vun, "Securing IoT for smart home system", *In 2015 International Symposium on Consumer Electronics ISCE,* IEEE, pp. 1-2, 2015.
        [http://dx.doi.org/10.1109/ISCE.2015.7177843]

[4]   D. Geneiatakis, I. Kounelis, R. Neisse, I. Nai-Fovino, G. Steri, and G. Baldini, "Security and privacy issues for an IoT based smart home", *In 2017 40th International Convention on Information and Communication Technology, Electronics and Microelectronics (MIPRO),* IEEE, pp. 1292-1297, 2017.
        [http://dx.doi.org/10.23919/MIPRO.2017.7973622]

[5]   R.Y. Endra, A. Cucus, and F.N. Affandi, "The concept and implementation of smart room using internet of things (IoT) for cost efficiency and room security", *J. Phys. Conf. Ser.,* vol. 1381, no. 1, p. 012018, 2019. []. IOP Publishing.].
        [http://dx.doi.org/10.1088/1742-6596/1381/1/012018]

[6]   J. Shen, C. Wang, T. Li, X. Chen, X. Huang, and Z.H. Zhan, "Secure data uploading scheme for a smart home system", *Inf. Sci.,* vol. 453, pp. 186-197, 2018.
        [http://dx.doi.org/10.1016/j.ins.2018.04.048]

[7]   F. Li, Z. Wan, X. Xiong, and J. Tan, "Research on sensor-gateway-terminal security mechanism of smart home based on IOT", In: *Internet of Things.* Springer: Berlin, Heidelberg, 2012, pp. 415-422.
        [http://dx.doi.org/10.1007/978-3-642-32427-7_58]

[8]   A. Tewari, and B.B. Gupta, "Cryptanalysis of a novel ultra-lightweight mutual authentication protocol for IoT devices using RFID tags. The Journal of Supercomputing, 73(3), 1085-1102. Singh, M. K., Kumar, S., & Nandan, D. (2023). Faulty voice diagnosis of automotive gearbox based on acoustic feature extraction and classification technique", *J. Eng. Res.,* vol. 11, no. 2, p. 100051, 2017.

[9]   D. Nandan, M.K. Singh, S. Kumar, and H.K. Yadav, "Speaker identification based on physical variation of speech signal", *TS Trait. Signal,* vol. 39, no. 2, pp. 711-716, 2022.
[http://dx.doi.org/10.18280/ts.390235]

[10]   M.K. Singh, "A text independent speaker identification system using ANN, RNN, and CNN classification technique", *Multimedia Tools Appl.,* vol. 83, no. 16, pp. 48105-48117, 2023.
[http://dx.doi.org/10.1007/s11042-023-17573-2]

[11]   M.K. Singh, "Feature extraction and classification efficiency analysis using machine learning approach for speech signal", *Multimedia Tools Appl.,* vol. 83, no. 16, pp. 47069-47084, 2023.
[http://dx.doi.org/10.1007/s11042-023-17368-5]

[12]   V. Satyanarayana, "Brain-computer interfaces interpret EEG data to determine mental state", *In 2023 3rd International Conference on Advancement in Electronics & Communication Engineering AECE,* IEEE, pp. 982-985, 2023.

[13]   M.K. Singh, P.M. Satya, V. Satyanarayana, and S. Gamini, "Speaker recognition assessment in a continuous system for speaker identification", *Int. J. Electr. Electron. Res.,* vol. 10, no. 4, pp. 862-867, 2022.
[http://dx.doi.org/10.37391/ijeer.100418]

[14]   K. Fan, P. Song, and Y. Yang, "ULMAP: Ultralightweight NFC mutual authentication protocol with pseudonyms in the tag for IoT in 5G", *Mob. Inf. Syst.,* vol. 2017, pp. 1-7, 2017.
[http://dx.doi.org/10.1155/2017/2349149]

[15]   M.K. Singh, M. Vyshnavi, S. Kumar, V. Satyanarayana, and H.K. Yadav, "Eradicating the scare consequences on IMC architecture", *In 2023 3rd International Conference on Advancement in Electronics & Communication Engineering AECE,* IEEE, pp. 977-981, 2023.
[http://dx.doi.org/10.1109/AECE59614.2023.10428377]

[16]   M.K. Singh, S. Manusha, K.V. Balaramakrishna, and S. Gamini, "Speaker identification analysis based on long-term acoustic characteristics with minimal performance", *Int. J. Electr. Electron. Res.,* vol. 10, no. 4, pp. 848-852, 2022.
[http://dx.doi.org/10.37391/ijeer.100415]

[17]   G. Ramadevi, G. Ajay Sankar, and M.K. Singh, "Role of IoT in intelligent agriculture network system. Advanced production and industrial engineering", *Proceedings of ICAPIE,* vol. 2022, no. 27, p. 218, 2022.

[18]   S. Kumar, D. Nandan, M.K. Singh, and R. Kumar, "A multiple band-notched monopole antenna with incorporated GSM and UWB for wireless applications", *Inter. J. Adv. Sci. Technol,* vol. 28, no. 16, pp. 362-378, 2019.

[19]   K.R.S. Reddy, C. Satwika, G. Jaffino, and M.K. Singh, "Monitoring of infrastructure and development for smart cities supported by IoT method", *Proceedings of Second International Conference in Mechanical and Energy Technology: ICMET 2021,* pp. 21-28, 2022.

[20]   C. Gu, C.H. Chang, W. Liu, S. Yu, Y. Wang, and M. O'Neill, "A modeling attack resistant deception technique for securing lightweight-PUF-based authentication", *IEEE Trans. Comput. Aided Des. Integrated Circ. Syst.,* vol. 40, no. 6, pp. 1183-1196, 2021.
[http://dx.doi.org/10.1109/TCAD.2020.3036807]

CHAPTER 7

Channel Response Measurements and Analysis of the Human Body for Biometric Resolutions

Mahesh K. Singh[1,*], **B.S. Kiruthika Devi**[2], **M. S. Priya**[1], **V. Satyanarayana**[1] and **Sanjeev Kumar**[1]

[1] *Department of ECE, Aditya University, Surampalem, India*

[2] *School of Computing, Sathyabama Institute of Science and Technology, Chennai, India*

Abstract: The infrastructure and technologies of computer security have undergone several improvements and modifications. There is a growing trend toward building an identity based on a combination of three factors: what you know, what you have, and who you are in the present (biometrics). Knowledge-based and token-based authentication systems have been deemed inadequate; however, new technology from the East has overcome these issues (biometrics). There is a chance that you will lose access to your resources if you forget your password. Biometrics is the science of identifying a person without disclosing private information. Biometrics is an authentication mechanism that uses a person's unique biological characteristics. This article examines the history and evolution of the many biometric identification modalities and the distinguishing characteristics that each of them possesses. The ability to recognize faces is one of the most fundamental ways in which humans have linked as individuals. Facial recognition is a sort of visual processing that works with human data. As there were no mirrors available to ancient humans, facial descriptions were typically established through the gaze of another person or, at best, through the description of the person's reflection in clear water. This was the normal practice for an extended period of time.

Keywords: Biometrics, Channel response, Distinctiveness, Minutiae features, Verification.

INTRODUCTION

Today, digital systems control every facet of human life, allowing more individuals to get the services they need through a variety of channels. Personal identification of smart devices based on biometric recognition, which uses an individual's unique biological characteristics to verify their identity, has become a viable option in recent years [1, 2]. When opposed to more archaic approaches

* **Corresponding author Mahesh K. Singh:** Department of ECE, Aditya University, Surampalem, India; E-mail: mahesh.092002.ece@gmail.com

Ashwani Kumar, Mohit Kumar, Avinash Kumar Sharma & Yojna Arora (Eds.)
All rights reserved-© 2025 Bentham Science Publishers

like password-based user identification processes or ID cards, which are prone to forgery and loss, biometric systems have clear advantages in terms of usability, portability, and accuracy. Damage to or disclosure of inherent biometric information renders recovery impossible and may even lead to misidentification. The use of many biometrics at once, or in addition to other security measures like an electronic signature or a personal identification number, can result in a much higher level of safety [3, 4].

This process can be used to verify the user's identity on a portable device by physically touching it, an action that is easy and intuitive for users of all ages. One can use this method to verify the authenticity of their own devices [5]. Direct connections utilizing the user's keys to establish Bluetooth or Wi-Fi networks between IoT devices can also execute the authentication operation in parallel with the pairing process. The pairing procedure is quite similar to setting up a Bluetooth or Wi-Fi network, making it an achievable target [6, 7].

Our initial step was to create an experimental setup in which we could measure BCR reliably without altering any underlying biometric traits, and for this, we relied on the theory behind capacitive coupling-based electrical signal transmission in the body. The electric signals released by the GE (Ground Electrode) of the receiver that produce oscillations in the electric field formed between the GE and the SE (Signal Electrode) of the transmitter can be used to analyze the body channel's parameters. [8, 9]. In contrast to biometric authentication, which differentiates itself by focusing on the live person, forensics does not require the identification of a person in real time shown in Fig. (**1**).

The term "distinctiveness" describes how significantly an individual's biometric pattern deviates from the norm of the community as a whole. The clarity of the labelling improves as the degree of difference increases. Having a one-of-a-kind personality is a key component in reaching the pinnacle of uniqueness. If a biometric pattern has a low degree of uniqueness, it is likely to be shared by most people [10, 11]. The following is a case in point: The differences between the iris and retinal geometry are greater than those between the hand and finger geometry. The implementation helps determine the appropriate level of uniqueness and resilience [12, 13].

RELATED WORK

Thanks to his development of the Bertillon body measurement system, Alphonse Bertillon is often credited as the man who initiated the field of modern biometrics [14]. A biometric identity system was first mentioned in the 1800s in Paris, France, despite references to biometrics going back to the Babylonian Empire in the 500s B.C. This biometrics report is more recent than accounts that came before it in 500 B.C. [15]. In order to better categorize and evaluate criminals, Alphonse Bertillon developed a method that relied on precise body measurements [16]. Average classification accuracy was roughly 95.8%, with no obviously biased topic misidentifications using the kernel-based support vector machine. Receiver operating characteristic curve analysis further demonstrates that the suggested classifiers are robust against decision limits over a wide range of threshold settings [17]. Beginning in 1991, groundbreaking research into face detection opened the door to the possibility of real-time facial recognition. Turk and Pentland found that residual error might be utilized for face recognition while working with eigenface approaches. This development paved the way for the creation of robust, in-process automatic facial recognition [18].

Fig. (1). Biometric resolutions of the human body [1].

In 1992, the United States government officially launched the Biometric Consortium. The first conference of the Biometric Consortium took place in October 1992, with the help of the National Security Agency [19]. The Consortium received its charter in 1995 from the Security Policy Board, which has since disbanded. At first, the Consortium was closed off to non-governmental organizations and only allowed private businesses and universities to join as observers. The program for developing face recognition technology (FERET) began in 1993. The Facial Recognition Technology (FERET) evaluation was funded by the Defence Advanced Research Products Agency (DARPA) and the Department of Defence Counterdrug Technology Development Program Office from 1993 to 1997. It was carried out under the guise of a research study. In 1995, people were finally able to get their hands on the Iris prototype. The first commercially viable iris product is the result of a collaboration between the Defence Nuclear Agency and IrisScan [20].

The year 1996 marks the debut of hand geometry at the Olympic Games. One of the most visible applications of hand geometry to date took place at the 1996 Olympic Games in Atlanta. Physical entry to the Olympic Village was limited and monitored with the help of hand geometry devices during these competitions. Over 65,000 people were successfully enrolled in the system, which is a significant achievement. Nearly a million unique transactions were handled in just 28 days. In 1997, the industry's first comprehensive standard for interoperable biometrics was released. As the first widely available open standard for biometric interoperability, the Human Authentication API (HA-API) was an important step forward in the development of the industry. The National Security Agency (NSA) developed it with the goals of easing integration, allowing for interchangeability, and promoting vendor independence [21]. This cleared the path for future biometric standardization efforts and was a major milestone in the process of biometric providers collaborating to improve the market through standardization.

In 1999, academics began investigating the possibilities of biometrics and MRTDs interoperability. The Technical Advisory Group on Machine Readable Travel Documents (TAG/MRTD) of the International Civil Aviation Organization commissioned research into the "compatibility of existing biometric technology with the issuing and inspection system." The compatibility of current biometric technology with the issuing and inspection procedures will be investigated. This was the year that the First Vendor Test of Face Recognition Technology, or FRVT 2000, was accomplished. The Face Recognition Vendor Test was supported in 2000 by a number of United States federal entities. During the Free and Reliable Voting Technical Test in 2000, a sizable portion of the public evaluated available biometric technology (FRVT 2000). The first public demonstration of face recognition software occurred in 2001 during the Super Bowl in Tampa, Florida.

As part of the security preparations for the Super Bowl stadium in Tampa, Florida, a facial recognition system was implemented in January 2001 in an effort to prevent "wanted" individuals from entering the premises. During the rally, at least a dozen law-abiding sports fans were incorrectly recognized despite the fact that none of the "wanted" individuals were located.

In 2002, the Identification Services Committee assumed responsibility for the Palm Print Staff Paper. In April of 2002, the Identification Services (IS) subcommittee of the Criminal Justice Information Services Division (CJIS) advisory policy board received a study on palm print technology and the prospects of the Integrated Automated Fingerprint Identification System (IAFIS). A recent paper examined palm print technology and the prospects of an integrated automated fingerprint identification system (APB). The JWG has requested that the CJIS Division of the FBI give "strong support" in the form of design, cost estimation, and implementation of an integrated latent print capability for palms. In 2003, the federal government of the United States took the initial move toward centralizing its biometric activities. A Subcommittee on Biometrics has been established under the National Science and Technology Council to manage biometrics-related R&D, policymaking, public engagement, and international cooperation efforts [22].

In 2004, President George W. Bush issued an executive order to ensure that all federal employees and contractors had government-issued photo IDs. When he released Homeland Security Presidential Directive 12 (HSPD-12) in 2004, one of President George W. Bush's major aims was to create a national ID. This card should be issued by every federal agency with workers or contractors who require access to secure federal buildings or networks. American patent protection for the idea of iris recognition lapsed in 2005. This crucial US patent covering iris identification expired in 2005, opening the door for competitors to develop their own iris recognition algorithms and cash in on the expanding market. The iris identification patent held by Dr. Daugman's LRIS Codes implementation did not run out until 2011.

Since 2008, the United States government has been working to standardize the use of biometric databases. The creation of appropriate toolkits and algorithms for assessing the quality of fingerprint images and facial features has been finalized. Additionally, an algorithm was created to evaluate iris quality. In 2010, biometrics were implemented into the United States' national security system for the purpose of identifying terrorists. The fingerprint of a detainee at GITMO was found to be a perfect match with evidence taken from the site where the 9/11 attacks were planned. When evidence was retrieved from the other 9/11 sites, additional fingerprints were found and used in the investigation.

2011: The remains of Osama bin Laden were found and positively identified using biometric data. The Central Intelligence Agency (CIA) used DNA and facial recognition technology to identify Osama bin Laden's remains. After a delay, Apple finally started including fingerprint sensors in its consumer-focused mobile devices in 2013. There are a number of Apple products, including the iPad Air 2 and iPad Mini 3, as well as the iPhone 5S, iPhone 6, and iPhone 6 Plus, that have Touch ID. Touch ID is extensively embedded into iOS devices, allowing users to do things like unlocking their iPhones, buying content from Apple's digital media stores, and verifying their identity when making transactions through Apple Pay. As a competitor to Apple's Siri virtual assistant, Microsoft developed Cortana in 2015.

In 2020, what did the state of biometric verification look like? Biometric technology at that time was safe enough to warrant broad use, and applications that made use of biometrics were effective because the features they measure are difficult to fake. Hardware scanners are more than 99 percent effective, and algorithmic accuracy is only going to improve. This indicates that there are various kinds of biometrics, each with its own merits and drawbacks. Depending on your intended services and the desired level of security, you will need to make a decision. Ethics and the law must be taken into account while using biometrics. However, if this challenge can be surmounted, it may offer a reliable, safe, and straightforward method of identifying individuals [23].

METHODOLOGY FOR BIOMETRIC RESOLUTIONS

This is a speech-enabled personal productivity assistant that operates using voice commands and is powered by machine learning. An important step forward in the widespread adoption of biometric technology in the commercial sector was taken in 2018 with the introduction of the first MasterCard Biometric Card. Fingerprint and chip technology were used for the in-store verification method. Furthermore, a car with built-in facial recognition technology was also available. When a driver enters their Bytom electric vehicle, the doors unlock, and their profile is loaded immediately. Additionally, drivers have the ability to manipulate many features of the car through the use of hand gestures and voice instructions shown in Fig. (**2**) proposed method for biometric resolutions.

Motion Trajectories Extraction

The extraction of moving objects and their pathways from films with precision is of the utmost significance. To accomplish this, we need a model that can accurately recreate the three-dimensional motion of an item and can survive the effects of a wide range of external conditions. Our model must account for the recording device as an extra source of noise. The resulting blobs now represent the moving elements of the scene. However, if occlusions are present or if there is a high degree of resemblance between the objects and the backdrop, our results may be deceptive.

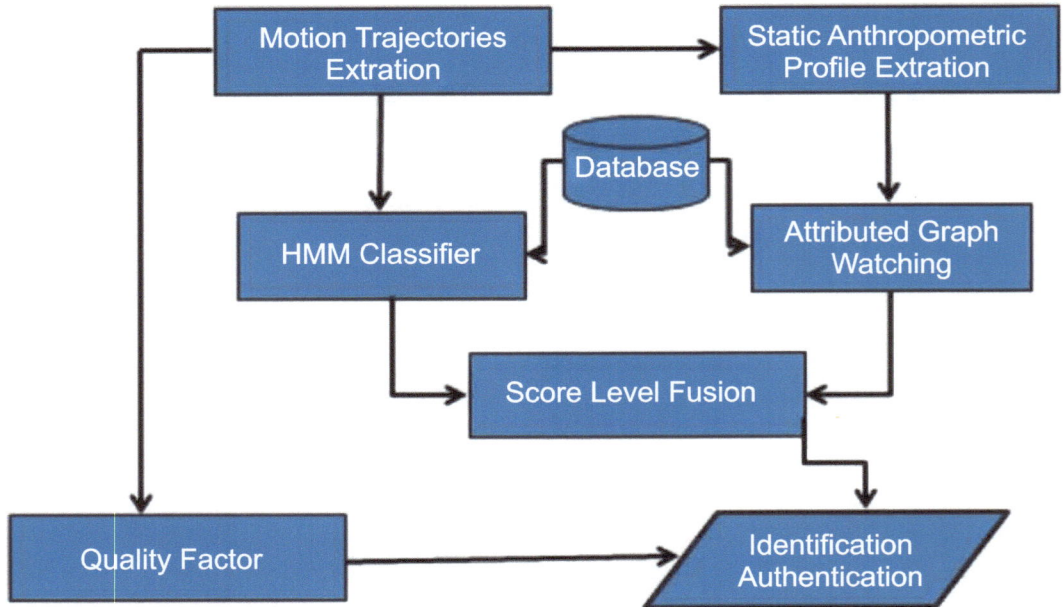

Fig. (2). Proposed method for Biometric Resolutions.

Extrapolation from an Anthropometric Profile Captured

Because of the ever-increasing demand for safety and surveillance in both public and private areas, the use of gait analysis as a form of biometric identification has experienced a meteoric rise in popularity over the past decade. Recent research conducted in multi-biometric environments has shown that gait could be a useful additional modality for biometric identification and authentication in the future. Identification of human gait is a challenging aspect of biometrics that is still in the process of being developed. Recognition rates can be affected by a variety of factors, including changes in view angle, clothing, footwear, surface, illumination, or stance.

HMM Classifier

Human gait recognition is an advanced and developing biometrics field. As we continue our investigation, we will be focusing on a specific aspect of HMM classification: the classification of two competing models. At first, we improve the architecture of the given HMMs so that we can tell when two different events lead to the same state. This is possible due to the data contained in HMMs. We show that our improved HMM retains the irreducibility and aperiodicity of its parent HMM (two conditions needed to apply Theorem 15). So, if you want to use Theorem 15, you need to meet these conditions. The augmented structure can recreate any state, down to the appearance, which is determined by the specifics of how that state was achieved shown in Figs. (**3** and **4**).

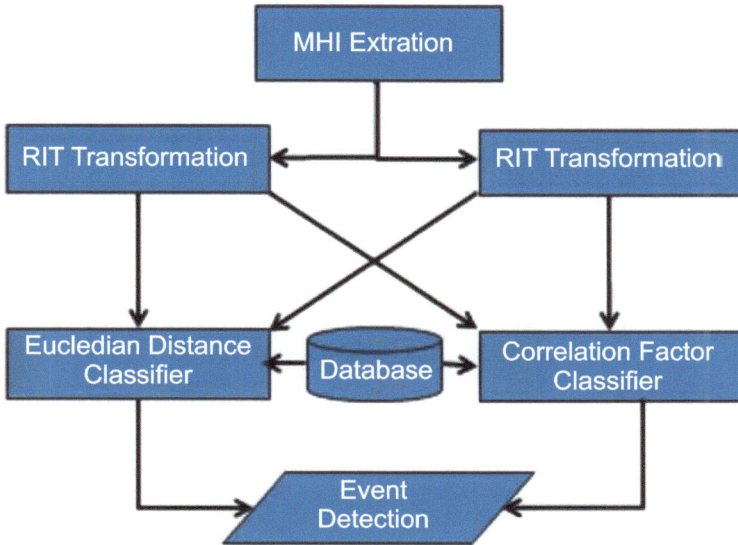

Fig. (3). Method for using a human body for biometric resolutions.

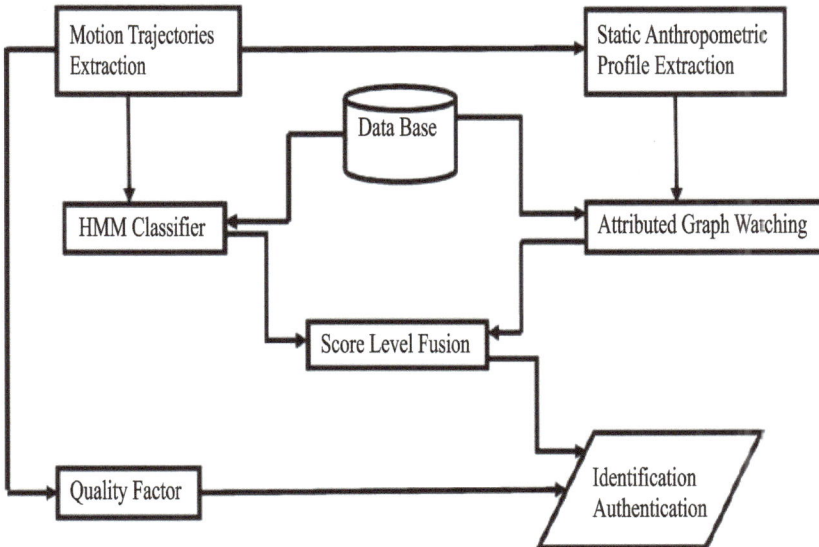

Fig. (4). Trajectory extraction for motion analysis.

Trajectory Extraction for Motion Analysis

A reliable method of extracting objects and their motion paths from video data is required. The process is known as motion trajectory extraction. We need to come up with a model that can hold up against the many different types of external stresses if we want to reproduce the motion of an object in three-dimensional space. Our model also needs to take into consideration any background noise that may have been introduced by the capturing mechanism. There are some blobs to stand in for the various objects in motion in the scene. However, occlusions or shared features of foreground and background may introduce errors in the information we collect.

Because of the growing importance of surveillance and security in both public and private spheres, gait as a biometric has got a lot of attention over the past decade. This has led to the development of a method for extracting a person's static anthropometric profile. Because of recent research in multi-biometric environments, walking has been developed as a possible identification and authentication modality.

RESULT AND DISCUSSION

A review of biometric user recognition techniques' dependability. This strategy is based on changes in HBIR caused by the idiosyncrasies of different sensory pathways. Using tailored pulse signals, the Human Body İnfrared (HBIR) signals of five individuals were recorded. The obtained data was then subjected to the specified signal processing in order to generate effective measures capable of differentiating subjects across the time, frequency, and wavelet domains. This study aimed to determine whether user recognition could be achieved in a residential setting utilizing HBIR. Due to the small number of participants in the study, it is not possible to extend the results to the general population. In fact, it is essential to ascertain how many users HBIR is capable of identifying, and this will be examined in subsequent research. Due to the oscilloscope's restricted sample rate capacity, activities at frequencies below 1 MHz were not examined. By raising the sample rate of the HBIR, a broader spectrum of behavioural and physiological characteristics can be collected.

This current investigation seeks to comprehend how precision improvement can profit from low-frequency data. In order to further examine some HBIR signals, we will develop specialized detection equipment that makes use of their unique qualities. Here, we evaluate the accuracy of a biometric user recognition system based on differences in HBIR caused by the unique properties of different human body channels. This technique employs a biometric. The HBIR signals of five individuals were recorded using five distinct impulse signals. Using the acquired data and the planned and executed signal processing, adequate measures for individual discrimination in the time, frequency, and wavelet domains may be generated, shown in Table **1** fusion performance at the feature level. The effectiveness of our method and the quality of the returned characteristics are both measured by how well they support recognition performance. We discovered in our research that the final identifier for each person is generated by a voting mechanism that includes four decisions based on four synthetic features of a single person. Furthermore, we compare the results obtained by extracting facial features from Low-Resolution (LR) photos versus High-Resolution (HR) images. As an example, Table **1** shows one outcome. Particular facial features extracted from high-resolution photos perform exceptionally well.

Table 1. Performance at feature-level fusion.

Fusion Method	Recognition Rate
HR Face and Gait	92.36%
LR Face and Gait	90.47%
Gait only	87.58%
HR Face Only	84.21%
LR Face Only	82.68%

In this work, we examined the viability of employing HBIR for user recognition in a small group, such as a family, but found that five participants were insufficient to account for all the physiological changes generated by HBIR. Future research will determine the number of users that HBIR can identify, as this is vital information. In addition, because of the sample rate limits of the oscilloscope, investigations of frequencies below 1 MHz were not conducted. If data collection occurs more frequently, the HBIR will be able to record a greater variety of physiological and behavioural parameters. As part of our ongoing research, we plan to investigate how low-frequency data can help increase precision. In addition, we will develop specialized sensor equipment to detect unique HBIR signals based on a range of identifying properties.

CONCLUSION

Soft biometrics include semantic human descriptions. Annotating a population with physical traits. It is confirmed in earlier studies about the most essential semantic elements. Semantic characteristics have identification potential, and integrating a gait biometric with them can improve accuracy. We plan to study semantic space. Comparing automated and semantic characteristics. These links enable automatic semantic annotations and content searches. We want to add physical appearance aspects to the semantic corpus. Crime scene witnesses often comment on a suspect's attire, piercings, or identifying marks, which might impact annotators' views even without a physical exam. Gait descriptions (such as shuffle, limp, or run), mood, subject goals, and social roles augment the dynamic components of gait compared to the static parts previously studied. Outliers, "strange" behaviour, location, and context affect how an issue is regarded. Questions such as, "Is this person misbehaving?" are context-dependent.

REFERENCES

[1]   C. Keroglou and C. N. Hadjicostis, "Hidden Markov model classification based on empirical frequencies of observed symbols," *IFAC Proc.*, vol. 47, no. 2, pp. 7–12, 2014.
[http://dx.doi.org/10.3182/20140514-3-FR-4046.00068]

[2]   J.L. Wayman, "The scientific development of biometrics over the last 40 years", In: *The History of Information Security.* Elsevier Science BV, 2007, pp. 263-274.
[http://dx.doi.org/10.1016/B978-044451608-4/50011-0]

[3]   Y. Jin, W.S. Soh, and W.C. Wong, "Indoor localization with channel impulse response based fingerprint and nonparametric regression", *IEEE Trans. Wirel. Commun.,* vol. 9, no. 3, pp. 1120-1127, 2010.
[http://dx.doi.org/10.1109/TWC.2010.03.090197]

[4]   Z. Yang, Z. Zhou, and Y. Liu, "From RSSI to CSI: Indoor localization *via* channel response", *ACM Comput. Surv.,* vol. 46, no. 2, pp. 1-32, 2013. [CSUR].
[http://dx.doi.org/10.1145/2543581.2543592]

[5]   J.L. Geisheimer, E.F. Greneker III, and W.S. Marshall, "High-resolution Doppler model of the human gait", In: *Radar Sensor Technology and Data Visualization.* vol. 4744. SPIE, 2002, pp. 8-18.
[http://dx.doi.org/10.1117/12.488286]

[6]   A. Pacut and A. Czajka, "Aliveness detection for iris biometrics," In: *Proc. 40th Annu. Int. Carnahan Conf. on Security Technology (ICCST)*, pp. 122–129, 2006.
[http://dx.doi.org/10.1109/CCST.2006.313440]

[7]   Y. Xie, Z. Li, and M. Li, "Precise power delay profiling with commodity WiFi", *Proceedings of the 21st Annual international conference on Mobile Computing and Networking,* pp. 53-64, 2015.
[http://dx.doi.org/10.1145/2789168.2790124]

[8]   M.K. Singh, S. Kumar, and D. Nandan, "Faulty voice diagnosis of automotive gearbox based on acoustic feature extraction and classification technique", *J. Eng. Res. (Ponta Grossa),* vol. 11, no. 2, p. 100051, 2023.
[http://dx.doi.org/10.1016/j.jer.2023.100051]

[9]   D. Nandan, M.K. Singh, S. Kumar, and H.K. Yadav, "Speaker identification based on physical variation of speech signal", *TS Trait. Signal,* vol. 39, no. 2, pp. 711-716, 2022.
[http://dx.doi.org/10.18280/ts.390235]

[10]   M.K. Singh, "A text independent speaker identification system using ANN, RNN, and CNN classification technique", *Multimedia Tools Appl.,* vol. 83, no. 16, pp. 48105-48117, 2023.
[http://dx.doi.org/10.1007/s11042-023-17573-2]

[11]   M.K. Singh, "Feature extraction and classification efficiency analysis using machine learning approach for speech signal", *Multimedia Tools Appl.,* vol. 83, no. 16, pp. 47069-47084, 2023.
[http://dx.doi.org/10.1007/s11042-023-17368-5]

[12]   M.K. Singha, D. Lavanyab, C.A. Madhuric, P. Rameshd, and V. Satyanarayanae, "Improving speech quality using deep neural network-based manipulation of cepstral excitation", *Proceedings of the First International Conference on Recent Developments in Electronics and Communication Systems*

(RDECS-2022), vol. 32, 2023p. 340
[http://dx.doi.org/10.3233/ATDE221279]

[13]   T.V. Devia, V. Satyanarayanab, and M.K. Singhc, "An efficient hybrid technique for automatic license plate recognitions", *Proceedings of the First International Conference on Recent Developments in Electronics and Communication Systems (RDECS-2022),* vol. 32, IOS Press., p. 180, 2023.
[http://dx.doi.org/10.3233/ATDE221255]

[14]   G. Ramadevi, G. Ajay Sankar, and M.K. Singh, "Role of IoT in intelligent agriculture network system. Advanced production and industrial engineering", *Proceedings of ICAPIE,* vol. 2022, no. 27, p. 218, 2022.

[15]   P.V. Padmaa, K. Varalakshmib, and M.K. Singhc, "Circuit analysis of multilevel converter for high-power applications. Advanced production and industrial engineering", *Proceedings of ICAPIE,* vol. 2022, no. 27, p. 194, 2022.

[16]   K.R.S. Reddy, C. Satwika, G. Jaffino, and M.K. Singh, "Monitoring of infrastructure and development for smart cities supported by IoT method", *Proceedings of Second International Conference in Mechanical and Energy Technology: ICMET 2021,* Singapore, pp. 21-28, 2022.India

[17]   K. Sushma, V. Satyanarayana, and M.K. Singh, "A copy and move image forged classification by using hybrid neural networks", *International Conference on Artificial Intelligence and Data Science,* pp. 101-111, 2021.Cham

[18]   M.P. Kalyan, D. Kishore, and M.K. Singh, "Local binary pattern symmetric centre feature extraction method for detection of image forgery", *International Conference on Artificial Intelligence and Data Science,* pp. 89-100, 2021.Cham

[19]   M.K. Singh, P.M. Satya, V. Satyanarayana, and S. Gamini, "Speaker recognition assessment in a continuous system for speaker identification", *Int. J. Electr. Electron. Res.,* vol. 10, no. 4, pp. 862-867, 2022.
[http://dx.doi.org/10.37391/ijeer.100418]

[20]   J.L.B. Ramos, Y. Li, and D. Huang, "Clinical and research applications of anterior segment optical coherence tomography – a review", *Clin. Exp. Ophthalmol.,* vol. 37, no. 1, pp. 81-89, 2009.
[http://dx.doi.org/10.1111/j.1442-9071.2008.01823.x] [PMID: 19016809]

[21]   M.K. Singh, KJ Sai Venkat Kaushik, Masabathula Sahithya, and G. Ajay Sankar. "Visual monitoring of many objects in real time using embedded GPU", *2023 International Conference on Advanced & Global Engineering Challenges (AGEC),* IEEE, pp. 50-54, 2023.
[http://dx.doi.org/10.1109/AGEC57922.2023.00021]

[22]   B.W. An, S. Heo, S. Ji, F. Bien, and J.U. Park, "Transparent and flexible fingerprint sensor array with multiplexed detection of tactile pressure and skin temperature", *Nat. Commun.,* vol. 9, no. 1, p. 2458, 2018.
[http://dx.doi.org/10.1038/s41467-018-04906-1] [PMID: 29970893]

[23]   R. Palaniappan, and D.P. Mandic, "Biometrics from brain electrical activity: a machine learning approach", *IEEE Trans. Pattern Anal. Mach. Intell.,* vol. 29, no. 4, pp. 738-742, 2007.
[http://dx.doi.org/10.1109/TPAMI.2007.1013] [PMID: 17299228]

CHAPTER 8

Applicability of AI in Cyber Security

Akshat Gautam[1,*], Esha Singh[1], Komal Shakya[1] and **Ajeet Kumar Sharma[1]**

[1] *Department of CSE, Sharda University, Greater Noida, India*

Abstract: Connectivity, data proliferation, and technology have gained great advantages in this age of digitization. However, these advantages bring significant cybersecurity challenges. Especially with the advancement of malware, phishing attacks, and ransomware, advances like these are making it challenging to stay ahead in traditional security practices.

The advanced complexity in cyber security arises from these developments, like cloud computing, the Internet of Things, and mobile technologies. Organizations now have to shield not only their traditional networks but also environments based on the cloud, endpoints, and third-party integrations. The more interconnected devices and systems grow, the harder they are to secure from Distributed Denial of Service attacks and data breaches, for instance. An important challenge would be the time it takes to detect and respond to cyber incidents. Traditional security systems rely on static rules or signature-based methods, which make them ineffective at changing attack tactics. Artificial Intelligence has emerged as one of the significant transformative elements within the realm of cybersecurity, offering improved methodologies for the detection, prevention, and alleviation of cyber threats. With the complexity and intricacy of cyberattacks on the rise, AI-driven systems offer a much more advanced system than conventional security approaches. Further, artificial intelligence can predict potential weaknesses and automate redundant security functions so that cybersecurity experts can focus on strategic matters. This chapter analyses the increasing role of artificial intelligence in the cyber defense strategy and its potential use in different sectors of security.

Keywords: Artificial intelligence, Cyber security, Cyber attack, Network security.

INTRODUCTION

Artificial Intelligence is changing the modern cyber security landscape to a great extent, as it improves threat detection and mitigation through increased efficiency in an accurate manner and speed. Cyber security systems become more responsive

---

[*] **Corresponding author Akshat Gautam:** Department of CSE, Sharda University, Greater Noida, India;
E-mail: ronitakki3@gmail.com

Ashwani Kumar, Mohit Kumar, Avinash Kumar Sharma & Yojna Arora (Eds.)
All rights reserved-© 2025 Bentham Science Publishers

and proactive against threats by leveraging machine learning, deep learning, and other AI techniques. The core work of AI includes automation of threat detection based on pattern and behavior learning of anomalies. Machine learning models can be trained on vast datasets so that they can spot suspicious activities and even deviations from the usual behavior [1]. Thus, a threat can be noticed and addressed much sooner than in the case of rule-based systems since the latter often do not possess such subtlety. AI also allows scalability for threat analysis due to the tremendous amount of data that would be involved with potential threats. This, in turn, reduces the burden on security teams, allowing them to focus on more complex issues and even predict potential cybersecurity threats before they emerge. This basis is laid on predictive analytics models that analyze historical data, laying out patterns that will lead to a security incident. Such models would outline vulnerabilities, predict the probability of an attack on a particular input, and provide methods for preventive measures. To enable real-time autonomous responses, AI must be properly utilized to detect the nature of threats and take appropriate actions, such as isolating infected systems, blocking malicious traffic, and applying patches to vulnerable areas. This autonomous response can significantly reduce the damage caused by malware attacks, especially when human intervention is delayed or insufficient.

Artificial intelligence is increasingly being used to help cyber defense systems adapt and evolve based on new information. It is challenging for traditional security tools to compete with the rapid evolution of threats in the cyber world, while AI systems are continually learning from new data and updating their models based on the new information; hence, these are very effective against APT. Cybercrime today uses automation, AI, and machine learning for optimal effectiveness and distribution of attacks [1]. Human factors are among the biggest challenges in cyber security as social engineering attacks exploit vulnerability by humans rather than technology. One of the reasons that most of these attacks is because of poor security practices, such as weak passwords and access controls and failure to update software.

The global nature of cyber threats indeed creates a challenge in terms of legal and regulatory frameworks, different from one country to another, respective to cyber security regulation. Moreover, the anonymity of the internet actually opens the opportunity for attackers to work from jurisdictions beyond law enforcement's reach. Indeed, achieving a good balance between robust security and budgetary constraints is a significant challenge, especially for SMEs.

The Role of AI in Addressing Cyber Threats

The current digital world needs real-time threats detection and ensures the safety and integrity of the systems. Because the nature and intensity of attacks are much more than conventional security solutions can capture, the detection and response to threats remain much delayed. Artificial Intelligence has indeed emerged as the game-changer that enables threat detection in real-time with a speed and accuracy one has never seen before.

This way, AI systems can scan humongous volumes of network traffic, user activity, and system behavior in real time because of the machine learning algorithms that identify anomalies when they occur. Due to comparisons in patterns of normal behavior, AI can rapidly spot anomalies that may be symptomatic of a cyberattack or unique login attempts, transfers of data, and application activities that sometimes surpass normal levels. Given such information, organizations can easily identify and neutralize potential threats before such threats become significant security breaches.

This is possible only if AI processes huge volumes of data, which might identify the subtle signs of an attack. Modern attacks are in the nature of APTs or zero-day exploits and are so designed to evade traditional security measures and go unnoticed for long periods. AI-based systems can track such subtle and hidden threats because such systems feed on new data continuously, adjusting models accordingly. Fig. (**1**) shows the flow chart attackers perform the attack.

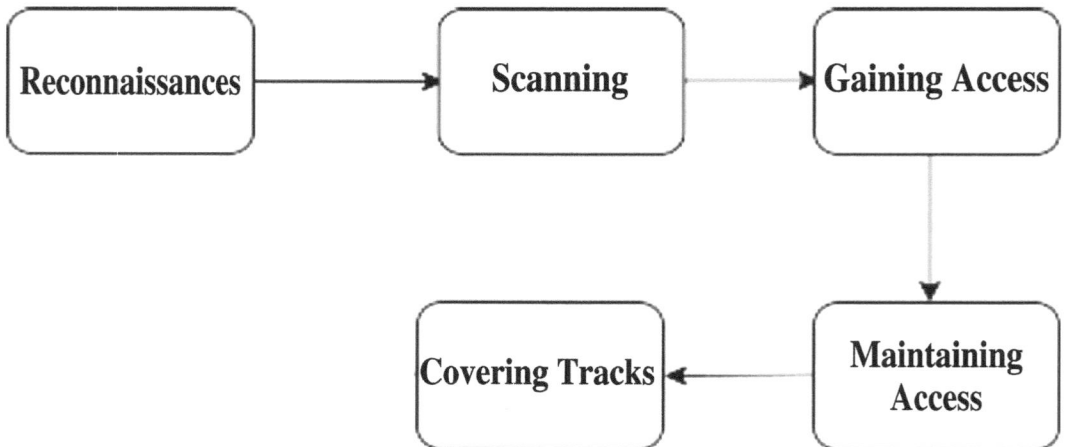

Fig. (1). Phases of attack.

For the systems to detect suspicious activities, they would start the response mechanisms automatically. This includes some network isolation, blocking some malicious IP addresses, and alerting the relevant security teams. Exposure windows and time that an attacker could use to exploit that vulnerability would thus be minimized, which is critical in reducing information loss, service disruption, and other risks.

AI escalates situational awareness through real-time insights into the threats, including their scope and severity, through predictive analytics and behavioral analysis. In attacks that are increasingly sophisticated and fast-changing, AI in its application concerning real-time detection of threats would never abate and would only increase to ensure organizations do not fall behind their adversaries but protect their digital assets with optimum assurance.

AI-Driven Threat Detection

Instead of static rules or predefined signatures, which may be outdated overnight, modern cyber threats demand more. One of the most powerful solutions to this problem is the detection of threats by AI-driven applications that identify potential threats at runtime using algorithms in machine learning, which goes beyond the standard proactive, adaptive, and intelligent capacity at risk detection through pattern, behavior, and anomaly analysis.

It trains a broad backbone of machine learning models and relies on big datasets, such as historical attack data, logs, normal network behavior, and systems, which are mainly used for detection in recognizing anomalous behavior in these systems. Models can identify possible deviations from expected behavior, including suspicious communication, unauthorized access attempts, or anomalous file transfers. Unlike any traditional systems, which rely on predefined attack signatures, an AI-based system will detect threats for which there has never been an instance in the past, especially in regard to zero-day attacks and APTs.

The most significant advantage AI provides in the detection process is the real-time processing of vast amounts of data. Large organizations gather massive amounts of information from various sources, and human analysts can't practically sift through those enormous sets of information. Fig. (2) shows how AI systems scan huge datasets in real time and identify the patterns that signal an attack.

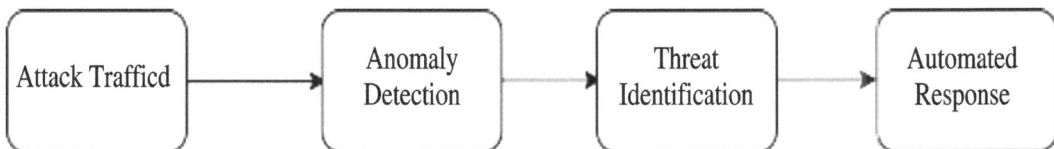

Fig. (2). AI-driven threat detection.

Another advantage of AI threat detection is that it generally prevents false positives commonly delivered by conventional security systems. It can further fine-tune the models for more precise detection in order to present fewer false alerts, allowing security teams to focus on real threats.

It can be integrated with Automated response mechanisms to make the threat detection systems more effective, like isolating compromised systems, blocking malicious traffic, or activating security protocols. This is a pretty fast and automated response that can pull down the destruction capability of cyberattacks so much because it diminishes the time between detection and mitigation so heavily. AI-based threat detection allows organizations to do proactive scalable and intelligent identification of cyber threats, which continuously learn from new data [2]. The value of an organization's ability to detect and neutralize before damage is done is increased by the contribution of constantly learning from new data and reduction of false positives for and driving automation responses.

AI in Malware Analysis

Malware is one of the most common and dangerous cyber threats; attackers come up with new versions of them, evading traditional detection systems. Because malware is continuously evolving, so it is the job of security teams to detect, analyze, and eliminate such threats. AI for malware analysis use cases brings a transformative approach that enables faster and more accurate detection as well as deeper analysis of malicious code [3, 4]. In short, the modern security solution can be processed by using and exploiting the techniques of machine and deep learning and other AI to identify newer threats, which might even predict future attacks. The most significant application of AI within the realm of malware analysis is perhaps that of machine learning related to malicious code classification. Traditional approaches, based on known signatures of malicious code, are rendered ineffective against newly designed or mutated forms of malware.

The AI-driven system follows the classification toward whether it is malicious or benign and, following the behavioral properties of the files, programs, or network activities, classifies malware for analysis. That would indeed mean zero-day threats could be detected because these pieces of malware have not been seen before. These can be static and dynamic analysis. Here, AI tools hasten the process of exhaustive analysis. For instance, in static analysis, an AI tool can speed up the scanning and deconstruction of files to identify suspicious code snippets and command families that are camouflaged or obfuscated. In the case of dynamic analysis, AI tools can monitor real-time behavior like changes to files, attempts to connect to external servers, and system calls. In practice, polymorphic malware and metamorphic malware alter their code with every new infection to ensure it is never detected. But AI will learn the underlying characteristics in which malware operates, hence identifying even the toughest, most hidden threats. Further, AI enhances malware prediction since predictive analytics is used in the formulation of trending malware. This will enable the security teams to predict new threats and take their defensive measures beforehand. In some AI-powered systems, they self-quarantine suspicious files; they will block malicious network traffic or recover from damage caused by malware.

Of course, cyber threat intelligence is related to AI, hence, data extracts from different sources related to malware can cross-correlate, including threat feeds, network logs, and global malware databases. This multi-dimensional knowledge regarding malware campaigns and morphs gives their security teams a better chance to build a defense strategy. Much will depend on AI for malware analysis as the threat landscape continues to evolve.

AI for Fraud Detection and Prevention

Frauds are the biggest concern in business, and with the pace at which digitized transactions and services continue to advance, fraud schemes evolve to be more sophisticated with a wide range of tactics. The more rule-based traditional systems of fraud detection, often with increasingly high human oversight, cannot manage the scale and complexity associated with some newer forms of attack. AI has brought powerful solutions using, among other avenues of machine learning, deep learning, and other techniques for accuracy, adaptability, and efficiency in detecting fraud [5].

The other major competitive edge that AI offers for fraud detection is the processing of massive volumes of transactions in real-time. Only with these volumes can the banking, e-commerce, and insurance industries process millions of transactions a day. Their large data sets can be processed by AI systems fast enough to detect patterns or anomalies in transactions that may lead to fraud. The AI model catches fraud in action since learning is continuous based on new data; hence, it ensures all apprehended threats are mitigated before causing any significant damage.

It means anomaly detection in fraud is indeed an important role of artificial intelligence. Machine learning algorithms are trained to identify normal transaction patterns, such as spending habits, geographical locations, and modes of payment. Once an outlier is detected AI notifies the organization for further investigation. Thus, real-time anomaly detection is made possible to prevent fraud from getting extended and protect the customer and business from their respective monetary loss. Another significant feature of fraud-detecting AI systems is their ability to learn and the versatility of various tactics of fraud. Fraudsters constantly develop new ways to achieve the same goals, often seeking novel methods to exploit system weaknesses. Rule-based systems get outrun by such changes since these rely on static rules that gradually remain outdated as time progresses. AI-based systems are dynamic and self-learning, continuously updating their models based on new patterns. As a result, they can detect emerging fraud tactics. AI also helps reduce false positives in fraud detection systems. Through better models with time, AI models identify trends and patterns where fraud is probable to occur in the near future so prevention can be made in time.

Biometric Security using AI

The progress in cyber threats has increased reliance on biometric security systems, especially facial recognition and iris scanning. Facial recognition is a biometric technology that uses advanced algorithms and deep learning to analyze facial features, offering greater reliability and security compared to older methods. AI-based facial recognition systems can identify and authenticate faces in real-time, even when partially occluded or in low-light conditions. With such an aspect of learning from new data, they are always able to improve their accuracy of identification and risk minimization of spoofing or face manipulation. This procedure for facial recognition is primarily divided into three stages: detection, feature extraction, and matching. Due to high precision in the process performed by AI, today it is very useful in various industries: law enforcement, airport security, and consumer electronics. Current systems also face challenges such as false positives and ethnic biases, issues that AI aims to address. Typically, traditional systems tend to be faulty in terms of the said issues, but AI-driven models can be trained from diverse datasets to improve fairness and reduce inaccuracies across demographics. Besides this, AI may find micro-expressions and other slight features that human eyes or non-AI systems would struggle to catch, thereby offering an added layer of security [6]. Another biometric method is iris scanning, which uses artificial intelligence to analyze the unique patterns in the colored part of the eye. Patterns found in an iris contain detailed features that can distinguish between persons hence making it one of the most reliable forms of biometric authentication. Iris scanning is related to AI-based iris-scanning technology. The advantages that this system possesses over others include an operative range in an extensive range of lighting conditions and the potential to authenticate people even from a distance. Besides, AI gives the system an edge to detect any artificial eyes or printed images, thereby not letting the process of scanning get spoofed. However, both facial recognition and iris scanning systems raise privacy concerns. Advanced biometric systems their basis in gathering sensitive data about the individual and storing that data, raising points of data security and consent. There are also misuses of the act of surveillance over public spaces, inasmuch as facial recognition can lead to mass surveillance of individuals without consent or even being aware of it [7]. The risk of those can only be assuaged by strong data protection measures and regulatory standards compliance when deploying an AI-driven biometric system by an organization. In conclusion, AI has revolutionized facial recognition and iris scanning technologies in the sense that they are not only more potent but also more accurate, reliable, and secure. That is to say; with deep learning algorithms, these systems authenticate people very rapidly and accurately in real-time; hence, they are highly valuable tools in a highly secure environment.

AI IN MULTI-FACTOR AUTHENTICATION (MFA)

Multi-factor authentication is a robust security system that adds to the authentication process of users using two or more related verification methods by which one or more relate to something the user knows, such as a password, something that the user has, such as a smartphone or token, and something the user is represented through biometric data, such as fingerprints or facial recognition. AI-driven technologies have emerged as the catalysts in changing the entire MFA efficacy, usability, and adaptability. This is because AI in MFA makes security and usability high-end through dynamic assessments of user behavior, identification of anomalous behavior, and risk prediction using advanced machine learning algorithms [8]. Traditional methods of MFA can get really cumbersome at times; they entail several steps that are likely to introduce delay or friction when trying to access services. It is designed in such a way that AI optimizes this by permitting the system to modulate the degree of verification based on the context of risk associated with each login attempt. Another area where AI is revolutionizing MFA is in behavioral biometrics. Instead of relying purely on static credentials, namely passwords or fingerprints, an AI-based system continuously monitors users' behavior during their interaction with a system. For example, the typing speed, mouse movements, and even the manner the user holds his device are profiled to create a unique behavior profile for each user. If there is any deviation from the profile, AI would be able to automatically trigger further steps of authentication. Real-time monitoring creates an important ability for MFA to function in the backseat without affecting usability or security [9]. Fig. (3) shows how AI can be utilized in multifactor authentication.

AI completely reduces credential theft and phishing attacks, as common in traditional authentication systems. AI can filter patterns of login attempts and thus prevent such attacks and keep accounts secure in the event of compromised login credentials. AI plays a key role in detecting and preventing fraud in MFA systems; it analyzes large amounts of data in real-time and identifies patterns of fraudulent behaviors on various platforms, accounts, and devices.

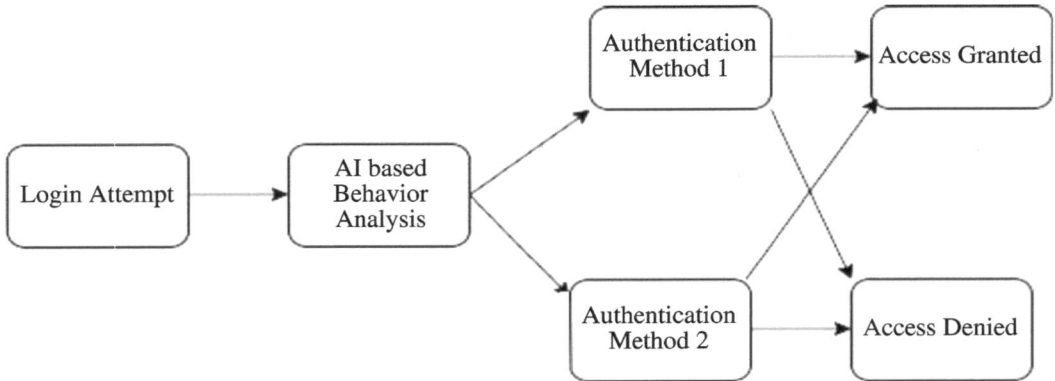

Fig. (3). AI in multifactor authentication.

Moreover, AI makes the MFA systems friendlier to the user as well, and authentication is much more intelligent and not overly bothersome. Of the innovations with AI, continuous authentication is one; it involves authenticating the user in the background while the user interacts with the system; it nullifies the myriad of MFA prompts within a session. AI-driven MFA plays a fundamental role in enhancing privacy by reducing the capture and storage of sensitive data. For an organization, the normal incident response methodologies have no match in today's fast-changing and highly sophisticated cyber threat landscape. Organizations are now looking for artificial intelligence-powered automated response systems so as to bolster their capabilities in the mitigation of threats [10, 11]. Such systems have the capability for real-time detection, analysis, and response, thereby preventing the potential impact of attacks and reducing the time taken for the response by several folds. Such AI-powered cybersecurity automation also makes the security posture stronger and frees the security team from time-consuming activities so that they can focus on complex ones. An automated response system, using AI algorithms, works out anomalies in huge volumes of data and executes predefined actions according to the threat gravity. For example, if an AI system detects network traffic anomalies resembling a DDoS attack, it can immediately block affected servers, redirect traffic, or apply rate limiting to mitigate the potential threat. The ML models that get trained on historic data from real attacks enable these systems to iteratively improve the accuracy of detection as well as make decisions more quickly. One of the most important aspects that automatic response brings in is in-time threat analysis. Traditional response techniques require human analysts to search through logs, correlate events, and assess risks before taking appropriate action. Automated AI-driven acceleration rapidly processes these data and correlates events within real time using advanced analytics and pattern recognition. For example, if there is a suspicious login attempt from a completely unknown location and the corresponding network activity is spiking, it could automatically flag this activity as a suspected breach and activate security, which may go so far as to block IP address, MFA prompt, or temporarily shut down vulnerable services. Another important aspect of automated response and threat mitigation is the use of playbooks. AI-enhanced automated systems can automate these playbooks without human interaction, thus allowing for quick and uniform responses. This way, orchestration through automation reduces the need to pull in human involvement and thereby effectively contains the threats. Another significant advantage of AI-driven automated response systems is that they continuously monitor and learn. They learn from the exposure to threats as the systems see new threats and, in doing so, update their threat models to adjust to emerging attack techniques. The dynamic learning capabilities of AI systems enable them to discover and respond to unfamiliar threats, commonly known as zero-day attacks, which traditional security measures have struggled to detect. Additionally, these systems have tremendous potential to reduce false positives. Security systems in legacy architectures simply overwhelm the analyst with the volume of data along with the lack of discrimination between legitimate threats and benign anomalies. AI systems can appropriately distinguish between actual attacks and mere noise, thereby sharpening their understanding of the normal behaviors within a network, thus increasing efficient response and eliminating alert fatigue.

AI IN VULNERABILITY SCANNING AND PATCH MANAGEMENT

Cybersecurity is one of the most important tasks involving discovering and remedying vulnerabilities in systems before they can be exploited by hackers. Traditional approaches such as manual scans, patching cycles, and response only leave a large amount of vulnerability opening since vulnerabilities are appearing in hundreds of thousands each year and increasing in complexity. AI is changing the game by providing accurate, proactive, and automated solutions to scan vulnerabilities and patch management [12, 13]. This kind of AI-based vulnerability scanning continuously scans the systems, networks, and applications for potential security weaknesses identified by sophisticated algorithms. The algorithms the systems utilize include those for machine learning that analyze large datasets in search of patterns; they can predict vulnerabilities that have not yet been documented. This capability enables the detection of zero-day vulnerabilities, flaws not yet identified or reported by the security community but still exploited by attackers. AI models can review the behavior of software components, predict anomalous patterns, and suggest potential vulnerabilities that would not have been discovered otherwise. AI-led systems can also conduct real-time scans to pick up changes or anomalies that may point to newly introduced vulnerabilities; this effectively reduces the time window for attackers to act on exploitation. It can also be integrated with threat intelligence feeds in order to pick on emerging vulnerabilities and attack vectors using global data, thus dynamically evolving the vulnerability scanning process to new threats will also orchestrate patch management across complex infrastructures, manage their deployment centrally across multiple platforms, and track the real-time patch status for every system. However, vulnerability scanning and patching through AI have their own sets of challenges that include false positives and adversarial attacks on AI models [14].

AI in Defending Enterprise Networks

Enterprise networks face persistent cyberattacks in the form of phishing scams, malware, and Advanced Persistent Threats (APTs). There are inadequacies in the traditional approaches to cybersecurity, which is why there is a need for a game-changer in the form of AI. AI technologies are in the form of machine learning and deep learning, which will aid in real-time threat detection, response, and network protection by automation and non-repetitive identification of patterns that are not possible with the analyst's identification. The given AI will pass through large amounts of data and filter through all that has been registered in a day for anomalies and security breaches [15]. This type of anomaly detection algorithm can notify unusual network behaviors that make the business respond faster and act accordingly. In IDS and IPS, AI-based solutions use their strongest machine learning algorithms for the identification of specific patterns in malicious activities across the network. They can identify known, but certainly unknown, threats, zero-day threats. So, these have been offering more solid security compared to static, rule-based systems. Another area in which AI excels for enterprise network security is with regard to behavioral analysis. AI is able to discern subtle signs of malicious activity while continuously monitoring the behavior of users, devices, and applications in detecting insider threats. AI can then amplify these response capabilities by automating incident management through device isolation, blocking the malicious sources' IP addresses, or, indeed, sending alerts to the security team.

Predictive analytics enables organizations to anticipate attacks before they occur by analyzing historical data and attack patterns, helping them stay one step ahead of attackers. Reliance on quality data to train AI models and adversarial attacks on AI models pose the main challenges [16]. The ongoing research in AI continues to improve the robustness and reliability of AI-driven security solutions.

AI and Quantum-Resistant Security

In rapid advancement, quantum computing has raised concerns for the cybersecurity world about breaking traditional cryptographic methods. Traditionally, techniques like RSA and ECC are based on problems such as factoring large prime numbers or calculations of discrete logarithms, which the application of quantum computers will do exponentially faster than any classical computer. This is a grave concern against modern-day security. It is now fast-tracked under the acronym of quantum-resistant security or Post-Quantum Cryptography (PQC). It aims to develop new methods of cryptography that would resist attacks from a quantum computer. Artificial intelligence is now increasingly playing a vital role in further accelerating quantum-resistant technologies and securing future systems against threats by quantum-powered cyber [17]. Quantum resistance in AI happens by auto-designing and testing new cryptographic algorithms, by analyzing such large sets of data, or by testing a number of encryption schemes, and they have been able to set patterns resistant to quantum attacks. This way, it can help an AI system optimize the amount of time and effort in this traditional process of developing a quantum-safe cryptography protocol. AI can also be applied to develop and apply improved encryption key management mechanisms with predictive security analysis for key distribution system vulnerabilities. Moreover, AI may be applied to implement quantum-resistant key exchange protocols. For instance, AI can create quantum-proof authentications such as biometric authentication that include face recognition, voice recognition, and iris scanning, making sure the whole process remains secured for user authentication in the post-quantum world. Moreover, AI can make use of quantum communication protocol optimization for the security of a network. However, this has limitations, since AI models are vulnerable to the impact of adversarial attacks besides requiring huge amounts of computational power. Integration of quantum-resistant algorithms is another key focus in the future of AI-driven security. Because quantum computers are now being designed and researched, many encryption methods will become insecure when attacked by these computer systems based on the principle of quantum technology. The future roadmap thus has to include developing and implementing quantum-safe cryptographic techniques so that AI systems can dynamically adjust to these new techniques. Collaborative AI models will have a big role in the future of security in terms of threat intelligence sharing across industries and nations. This would mainly require one to standardize and ensure interoperability of AI systems as part of policy development in cybersecurity and strategy. Human-AI collaboration will extend more rapidly with the advancement of AI technology. A highly probable spreading application of AI-driven security is required to ensure fairness, transparency, and accountability in sustaining the trust base in AI systems.

Cyber Resilience through AI-Driven Response Systems

Cyber resilience is one of the important elements of the security strategy and hence involves standing up against attacks and recovering quickly and adaptively. AI-driven response systems have a central role in enhancing cyber resilience by automating incident response, improving recovery processes, and providing fortification in defending against future threats [18]. AI-driven systems use machine learning algorithms for identifying patterns or signatures in an attack, assessing the level of threat, and actually triggering automated responses based on pre-defined security policies. With this level of automation, organizations are much more responsive to cyber events than they would be with human intervention. The most important contribution AI makes to cyber resilience is addictiveness. AI systems can learn from every cyber event, thus constantly refining their response strategy. For instance, in the case of a ransomware attack, AI would study the entry path, determine how the malware entered the system, and act swiftly with live countermeasures, such as isolation of the infected machines, shutdown of external communication channels, and further reinforcement of limitations in the spread of malware. They could also make recommendations for long-term security enhancements based on lessons learned from the attack, such as updating firewall rules, tightening access controls, or improving encryption protocols [19]. AI-based response systems may also facilitate automated remediation, that is, attempting to repair the vulnerabilities under which the attack occurred. These systems should be able to perform vulnerability scanning after a threat was neutralized, pointing out weaknesses in the infrastructure and, probably, suggesting what patches need to be installed, updating the software, or changing security configurations to close those security gaps that allowed the attack to happen. Such proactive remediation essentially reduces the probability that similar attacks might happen in the future and assists in ensuring that, over the long term, the organization stays secure and resilient.

AI in Building Self-Learning Cyber Defense Systems

The industry of cybersecurity is also increasingly using AI for more adaptive and intelligent mechanisms of defense. Innovative advancement has come about in self-learning cyber defense systems, as they adapt through AI to automatically learn, evolve, and improve over emerging threats. Such a paradigm is very different from previous approaches based on strictly defined or updated signatures for threat detection and mitigation. However, through these AI-powered systems, it will always be a data stream of continuous analysis, pattern recognition, learning new behaviors of attacks in real-time, and autonomously detecting and responding to the threats with no intervention. The main advantage of self-learning characteristics is that it enables real-time detection and response to threats. It can be trained on almost humongous volumes of network traffic, user behavior, and attacks from history and can detect subtle changes in network behavior that may indicate the presence of malicious activity. These self-learning systems are further augmented by deep learning algorithms, more so those that have appeared in the form of neural networks, to handle large quantities of data sourced from the internet, with the kind of applications such as firewall logs, IDS, and EDR platforms. AI-based systems can automatically respond using predefined policies or real-time data processing, making them highly effective at automating response mechanisms. For example, if a system has identified anomalous traffic that defines a DDoS attack, it can at once cut affected parts out of the network, block malicious IP addresses, or redirect traffic to lose the effects of the attack. The self-healing capability is particularly sensitive in large enterprises and massive infrastructures where downtime or data loss can be associated with huge economic consequences that may be incurred. AI has fantastic capabilities to parse and learn against an ever-changing threat landscape that makes it well-suited for new kinds of unknown malware and ransomware. Self-learning systems can monitor and analyze in real time how endpoint devices behave and detect any deviations that may indicate a compromise, such as unauthorized access or data exfiltration. Different application areas of AI are mentioned in Table 1.

Table 1. Applications areas of AI.

Application Area	AI Technology/Methodology	Benefits
Enterprise Network Security	Machine Learning, Anomaly Detection, Behavioral Analysis	Real-time threat detection, faster response to unusual network behaviors
Nation-State Cyber Defense	Threat Intelligence, Vulnerability Scanning, and threat attribution	Enhanced situational awareness, proactive threat mitigation
Intrusion Prevention and Detection	Autonomous AI-driven Systems	Automatically identifies and blocks malicious traffic
Fraud Detection	Neural Networks, Predictive Analytics	Prevention of fraud by analyzing user behavior and transaction patterns
Healthcare Cybersecurity	Anomaly Detection, Data Security Analytics	Protects sensitive medical records from unauthorized access
Defense and Military Applications	Data Analysis	Identifies and neutralizes threats by analyzing large data volumes

AI is transformative in building self-learning cyber defense systems, where an organization can be ahead of the game of cybercriminals by their continuous evolution in their defense.

CHALLENGES AND LIMITATIONS OF AI IN CYBER SECURITY

One of the key threats to developing AI models is the risk of adversarial attacks. An adversarial attack is an alteration of a small portion of the input data, which allows a state of deception of an AI system into producing an incorrect prediction or decision. This emerging threat means that there is an important implication for the security of AI-driven defenses since the attacker can exploit weaknesses in the very models that have been designed for protection from cyber threats. The method involves introducing carefully designed perturbations—slight changes to input data that may go unnoticed by humans but can cause AI models to malfunction. Added to an image, text, or even network traffic, these attacks can be disastrous. For example, a highly trained malware detection AI could be nudged toward incorrectly classifying a malicious file as innocuous, depending on how the adversary tweaks it in subtle ways that play on the AI model's blind spots. A small tweak of pixel values can not be perceived by the human eye, but an attacker could make use of it to evade facial recognition or impersonate a different person [20].

This remains a significant limitation of adversarial attacks, which rely on the learning processes of the AI models. Most AI models rely upon large datasets to make predictions based on observed patterns. Another concern is that AI systems can learn unwanted patterns or biases, including those introduced through adversarial manipulation. When such examples are introduced into the training or inference process, attackers can manipulate the model's behavior, leading it to perform incorrectly or unproductively.

One of the biggest concerns about adversarial attacks is scalability. For a lot of AI models, which are trained on large datasets or are being deployed in cloud environments, such weaknesses can be attacked at scale and exploited to affect multiple systems at once. Such threats exist in applications on a large scale, that as biometric authentication systems, intrusion detection systems, and network traffic analysis tools. Mitigating the risk of an adversarial attack requires the application of a multi-pronged approach. One such widely used technique is adversarial training, in which AI models are trained on both clean and adversarial-modified data to improve their robustness. Another technique is defensive distillation, in which the boundary decision of a model is attempted to be smoothed such that an adversary will have to make more effort to find a weakness in it. This would mean that the cybersecurity teams need to keep abreast of the constant evolution in the adversarial landscape in terms of continuous monitoring of AI performance, updates in defenses, and, even more, the evolution of models against emerging attack vectors.

Ethical Concerns in AI-driven Security

Artificial intelligence use in a cybersecurity framework triggers ethical concerns in terms of its deployment. These would include algorithmic bias, transparency, and autonomy, among others. One of the concerns is the potential for algorithmic bias that could undermine public trust in AI-driven security systems to work inaccurately as they either discriminate against certain individuals or detect nothing but create false positives [21].

- **Transparency**: This may sometimes become opaque with the ability of AI to make decisions and act upon them in real time. The transparency could not be understood or interpreted by humans regarding those decisions. This induces the black box problem, where users blindly trust the AI without understanding its rationale.
- **Autonomy:** AI systems can autonomously start making decisions and act them out in real-time; this may induce over-reliance on AI and potential misuse of data. With the wrong kind of hands under its control, AI can be used for launching sophisticated cyber-attacks, large-scale surveillance or cyber espionage. The more powerful the AI becomes, the more questions arise in regard to who controls these technologies and how they are used, especially when AI systems may infringe on personal freedoms or monitor individuals without consent.
- **Privacy:** The issue of privacy, ownership of data, and consent is one other concern raised by the integration of AI with biometric systems. Widespread collection, storage, and the possibility of abusing or breaching biometric data may not be within the control of an individual. That is why the high intrusiveness of biometric technologies into everyday life makes it a question of security *vs* privacy.

It becomes increasingly clear that addressing these ethical concerns requires regulation and ethical guidelines to govern the use of AI in cybersecurity. Ethical development of AI should ensure fairness, transparency, and accountability in the preparation of AI systems that observe human rights and ethical principles. Just treatment of AI in security applications stipulates the need for organizations possessing AI systems that tend to have an undue effect either on groups of people or even on certain individuals. It will surely be balancing AI automation with human control that will help AI-run security systems remain ethical and accountable.

CONCLUSION

The rise of sophisticated cyber threats led to the great rise of Artificial Intelligence because it is very relevant and indispensable in being used within cybersecurity, and it is clear that the traditional systems based on predefined rules as well as human intervention cannot cope with such dynamic modern attacks. AI is uniquely suited to process vast volumes of information and identify delicate patterns with such a challenge in real-time. Real-time AI cybersecurity systems are modifying the capabilities of organizations toward detecting, preventing, and reacting to threats. AI models are capable of learning from new data in continuous trends, so it allows the system not to stand still and be static based on rules but adapt evolving attack strategies. Machine learning algorithms would be able to detect unknown malware and zero-day vulnerabilities by tracing network traffic and system activities, which increasingly is becoming a must as cybersecurity moves toward a universally bound global concern. In this direction, the requirement for advanced and scalable, intelligent solutions means that with more nation-state attacks, cyber threats against infrastructure, and other vulnerabilities cutting across borders, AI offers real-time situational awareness and dynamic decision-making supplemented by automated defense responses that human operators alone cannot hope to achieve at scale. Furthermore, the complete penetration of AI into cybersecurity may probably create surveillance systems that violate civil liberties. An ethical responsibility needs to be fulfilled so that the application of AI in cybersecurity is fair and respects human rights. Conclusion AI has a vast potential for revolutionizing cybersecurity, but one needs to be cautious and careful about the application so that its consequences do not become undesirable. Fast-emerging technologies are rapidly upgrading the world of cybersecurity, but they also bring some ethical challenges. Artificial Intelligence raises a concern regarding the issue of data privacy. Heaps of personal and sensitive information may be collected by some AI systems so that they might infringe on the privacy rights of individuals. Organizations need to implement privacy by design principles such that designing an AI system ensures minimized data collection with good access controls and restraints. Another ethical issue is the transparency and accountability of AI algorithms; most AI systems presently work as black boxes, meaning one cannot make any sense of their way of making decisions. The very use of such AI when sensitive security decisions are left to them is problematic. The solution lies in explainable AI (XAI) models, which provide clear and detailed explanations of their decision-making processes.

REFERENCES

[1]   K. Sharma, and R. Kumar, "A comprehensive survey of DDoS attacks: Evolution, mitigation and emerging trend", *2024 3rd International conference on Power Electronics and IoT Applications in Renewable Energy and its Control PARC,* pp. 185-188, 2024.
[http://dx.doi.org/10.1109/PARC59193.2024.10486696]

[2]   Z. Zhang, H.A. Hamadi, E. Damiani, C.Y. Yeun, and F. Taher, "Explainable artificial intelligence applications in cyber security: State-of-the-art in research", *IEEE Access,* vol. 10, pp. 93104-93139, 2022.
[http://dx.doi.org/10.1109/ACCESS.2022.3204051]

[3]   V.D. Soni, "Challenges and solution for artificial intelligence in cybersecurity of the USA", *SSRN,* 2020.
[http://dx.doi.org/10.2139/ssrn.3624487]

[4]   A. Carlo, "The importance of cybersecurity frameworks to regulate emergent AI technologies for space applications", *J. Space Saf. Eng.,* vol. 10, no. 4, pp. 474-482, 2023.
[http://dx.doi.org/10.1016/j.jsse.2023.08.002]

[5]   M. Binhammad, S. Alqaydi, A. Othman, and L.H. Abuljadayel, "The role of AI in cyber security: Safeguarding digital identity", *J. Inf. Secur.,* vol. 15, no. 2, pp. 245-278, 2024.
[http://dx.doi.org/10.4236/jis.2024.152015]

[6]   I.H. Sarker, M.H. Furhad, and R. Nowrozy, "AI-driven cybersecurity: An overview, security intelligence modeling and research directions", *SN Comput. Sci.,* vol. 2, no. 3, p. 173, 2021.
[http://dx.doi.org/10.1007/s42979-021-00557-0] [PMID: 33778771]

[7]   A. Gurtu, "How AI will transform the cyber security industry", *Netw. Secur.,* vol. 2022, no. 1, 2022.
[http://dx.doi.org/10.12968/S1353-4858(22)70002-5]

[8]   A.J.G. de Azambuja, C. Plesker, K. Schützer, R. Anderl, B. Schleich, and V.R. Almeida, "Artificial intelligence-based cyber security in the context of industry 4.0—a survey", *Electronics (Basel),* vol. 12, no. 8, p. 1920, 2023.
[http://dx.doi.org/10.3390/electronics12081920]

[9]   M. Malatji, and A. Tolah, "Artificial intelligence (AI) cybersecurity dimensions: a comprehensive framework for understanding adversarial and offensive AI", *AI Ethics,* no. Feb, 2024.
[http://dx.doi.org/10.1007/s43681-024-00427-4]

[10]   D. Alsadie, "Artificial intelligence techniques for securing fog computing environments: trends, challenges, and future directions", *IEEE Access,* vol. 12, pp. 151598-151648, 2024.
[http://dx.doi.org/10.1109/ACCESS.2024.3463791]

[11]   F. ALmojel, and S. Mishra, "Advancing hospital cybersecurity through IoT-enabled neural network for human behavior analysis and anomaly detection", *Int. J. Adv. Comput. Sci. Appl.,* vol. 15, no. 5, 2024.
[http://dx.doi.org/10.14569/IJACSA.2024.0150506]

[12]   A. Alnaffar, "Cybersecurity resilience awareness in the Era of AI", *Int. J. Sci. Res. (Raipur),* vol. 13, no. 3, pp. 244-245, 2024. [IJSR].
[http://dx.doi.org/10.21275/SR24305145928]

[13]   M.S. Araujo, B.A.S. Machado, and F.U. Passos, "Resilience in the context of cyber security: A review of the fundamental concepts and relevance", *Appl. Sci. (Basel),* vol. 14, no. 5, p. 2116, 2024.
[http://dx.doi.org/10.3390/app14052116]

[14]   W. Salhab, D. Ameyed, F. Jaafar, and H. Mcheick, "A systematic literature review on AI safety: Identifying trends, challenges, and future directions", *IEEE Access,* vol. 12, pp. 131762-131784, 2024.
[http://dx.doi.org/10.1109/ACCESS.2024.3440647]

[15]   K. Zkik, A. Belhadi, S. Kamble, M. Venkatesh, M. Oudani, and A. Sebbar, "Cyber resilience framework for online retail using explainable deep learning approaches and blockchain-based consensus protocol", *Decis. Support Syst.,* vol. 182, p. 114253, 2024.
[http://dx.doi.org/10.1016/j.dss.2024.114253]

[16]   C.J. Chung, "Preservice teachers' perceptions of AI in education", *AI-EDU Arxiv.* no. May, pp. 1-5, 2024.
[http://dx.doi.org/10.36851/ai-edu.vi0.4155]

[17]   A. Habbal, M.K. Ali, and M.A. Abuzaraida, "Artificial intelligence trust, risk and security management (AI TRiSM): Frameworks, applications, challenges and future research directions", *Expert Syst. Appl.,* vol. 240, p. 122442, 2024.
[http://dx.doi.org/10.1016/j.eswa.2023.122442]

[18]   K. Sharma, and R. Kr, "A comprehensive survey of various cyber attacks", *2023 6th Int. Conf. Inf. Syst. Comput. Netw. ISCON,* pp. 1-4, 2023.
[http://dx.doi.org/10.1109/ISCON57294.2023.10111998]

[20] M.N.A.L. Al Waro'i, "Enhancing security through intelligent threat detection and response: The integration of artificial intelligence in cyber-physical systems", *Secur. Intell. Terror. J. (SITJ),* vol. 1, no. 1, pp. 1-11, 2024. [SITJ].
[http://dx.doi.org/10.70710/sitj.v1i1.1]

[21] S. Alnutefy, and A. Alsuwayh, "Unsupervised anomaly detection", *AI, Machine Learning and Applications,* no. Jan, pp. 145-154, 2024.
[http://dx.doi.org/10.5121/csit.2024.140210]

[22] M.H. Behiry, and M. Aly, "Cyberattack detection in wireless sensor networks using a hybrid feature reduction technique with AI and machine learning methods", *J. Big Data,* vol. 11, no. 1, p. 16, 2024.
[http://dx.doi.org/10.1186/s40537-023-00870-w]

SUBJECT INDEX

Ashwani Kumar, Mohit Kumar, Avinash Kumar Sharma & Yojna Arora (Eds.)
All rights reserved-© 2025 Bentham Science Publishers

www.ingramcontent.com/pod-product-compliance
Lightning Source LLC
Chambersburg PA
CBHW041444210326
41599CB00004B/133